TORONTO MEDIEVAL LATIN TEXTS 34

TORONTO MEDIEVAL LATIN TEXTS

THE DISPUTATIO PUERORUM

A NINTH-CENTURY MONASTIC INSTRUCTIONAL TEXT

Edited from

Vienna, Österreichische Nationalbibliothek, 458

by

ANDREW RABIN

and

LIAM FELSEN

Published for the

CENTRE FOR MEDIEVAL STUDIES

by the

PONTIFICAL INSTITUTE OF MEDIAEVAL STUDIES

Toronto

Library and Archives Canada Cataloguing in Publication

Disputatio puerorum
The Disputatio puerorum : a ninth-century monastic instructional text / edited from Vienna, Österreichische Nationalbibliothek, 458 ; by Andrew Rabin and Liam Felsen.

(Toronto medieval latin texts ; 34)
This volume is based on the A-recension of the Disputatio, Vienna, Österreichische Nationalbibliothek, 458.
Includes bibliographical references and index.
Issued in print and electronic formats.
Text in Latin with introduction and notes in English.
ISBN 978-0-88844-484-4 (softcover).–ISBN 978-1-77110-385-5 (PDF)

1. Disputatio puerorum. 2. Carolingians – Education – Sources. 3. Education, Medieval – Sources. 4. Learning and scholarship – History – Medieval, 500–1500 – Sources. 5. Monastic and religious life – History – Middle Ages, 600–1500 – Sources. 6. Manuscripts, Medieval. 7. Österreichische Nationalbibliothek. Manuscript. 458. I. Rabin, Andrew, editor II. Felsen, Liam, 1971–, editor III. Pontifical Institute of Mediaeval Studies, issuing body IV. Österreichische Nationalbibliothek. Manuscript. 458 V. Title. VI. Series: Toronto medieval Latin texts ; 34

LA91.D57 2017 370.9'02 C2017-903176-7
C2017-903177-5

The Pontifical Institute of Mediaeval Studies
59 Queen's Park Crescent East
Toronto, Ontario, Canada M5S 2C4
www.pims.ca

MANUFACTURED IN CANADA

PREFACE

The TORONTO MEDIEVAL LATIN TEXTS series is published for the Centre for Medieval Studies, University of Toronto, by the Pontifical Institute of Mediaeval Studies. The series offers affordable editions suitable for university-level courses in medieval Latin. In approving projects, the editorial board bears in mind the pedagogical utility of the texts proposed.

At the same time, the series also aims to further original research by publishing previously unedited texts extant in single manuscripts, as well as more widely attested texts here edited from single manuscripts carefully chosen for their particular textual, historical, and codicological interest and importance, in recognition that the scribal makers of such versions were important participants in the ongoing development of the text. Throughout the series, the base manuscript is emended only to restore sense, not to reconstruct an original authorial version; the minimal textual apparatus omits variants irrelevant to the integrity of the selected manuscript. Manuscript orthography and syntax are carefully preserved.

The Editorial Board, beyond merely supervising, takes responsibility for reviewing all proposals, for examining all specimens of volume editors' work, and for final reading of all editions published. It decides on all matters of editorial policy.

As General Editor, I would like to express my gratitude to the Centre for Medieval Studies for sponsorship of the series; to the Press of the Pontifical Institute and its unfailingly cordial and astute staff, particularly Fred Unwalla; to A.G. Rigg, whose sustained and tireless work as General Editor of the series for its first thirty volumes set a daunting standard to emulate; to Anna Burko, whose care and precision as Editorial Assistant did so much to maintain the standards of the series for over thirty years; to Philippa Matheson, whose expert work as Associate Editor continues so reassuringly to support the series. Finally, I am deeply indebted to all members of the editorial board, past and present, for the generosity of their sustained involvement, without which the series could not exist.

D.T.

ACKNOWLEDGMENTS

The questions and answers that make up the *Disputatio puerorum* have provided considerable inspiration for the editors, who have sought out the insight and assistance of many people in the course of producing this volume. We are especially grateful to Professors David Townsend of the University of Toronto and Erika Kihlman of Stockholm University. We deeply appreciate both their patience with us and their support for the project. Their assiduous readings of each draft of the manuscript saved us from more embarrassing errors than we can count—and certainly more than we'd like to admit. Errors that remain are, of course, our own. We are likewise grateful to Professors Martha Bayless and James Earl of the University of Oregon, and to Professors Thomas Maloney, Blake Beattie, Pamela Beattie, and Glynis Ridley of the University of Louisville. They have been as generous with their wisdom and time as the *magister* of the *Disputatio*. We hope our efforts have done them justice.

Additional thanks are due to the librarians and staff of Hill Museum and Manuscript Library in Collegeville, Minnesota, the Österreichische Nationalbibliothek in Vienna, the Russian National Public Library in St. Petersburg, the Bayerische Staatsbibliothek in Munich, and the Robarts Library at the University of Toronto. Their help in answering questions and providing microfilms and facsimiles has been crucial to the success of this volume.

Finally, the editors would like to thank their families for their patience as this project moved towards completion. We dedicate this volume to our own *pueri*: Tiana and Zachary Felsen, and Ari and Eli Rabin.

A.R. and L.F.

CONTENTS

INTRODUCTION

> Theology, spirituality, cultural history: these three realities were not separated in the real life of the monks, and they can never be dissociated.[1]

> From the beginning of the monastic movement, monks tried to fashion for themselves an original educational program. All the diverse activities of monastic life—prayer, the liturgy, reading, manual labor—had but one goal: the total transformation of the culture and habits of the men who left the world for the monastery.[2]

In describing the features of an early medieval monastic education, Jean Leclerq and Pierre Riché both point to the same underlying principle: that full immersion in the holy life of the cloister demanded a systematic understanding of both the natural world and its connection to the spiritual realities of the Bible. For the novice monk, the goal of his training was not merely knowledge of the Gospels and the orthodoxies of the Church. Rather, he sought to understand how the elements of his immediate experience—the state of his physical body, the composition of nature, and the steady progress of time—fit into a coherent Christian worldview, one in which the monastery marked a crucial intersection between this world and the next. Yet an education of this sort posed significant practical challenges for monastic schoolmasters. Although the corpus of human knowledge had been collected, systematized, and integrated with Christian orthodoxy by scholars and theologians such as Isidore of Seville and the Venerable Bede, their texts were often too unwieldy for novices early in their education and with only a limited grasp of Latin. The solution took the form of compilations of excerpts reworked into textbooks and simplified for the use of beginning students. These primers distilled the essence of canonical texts

1 Jean Leclerq, *The Love of Learning and the Desire for God: A Study of Monastic Culture* (New York, 1961), 6.

2 Pierre Riché, *Education and Culture in the Barbarian West from the Sixth through the Eighth Centuries*, trans. John Contreni (Columbia, 1976), 100.

into digestible units that made the teachings of the Church accessible while also highlighting those elements of Christian doctrine deemed most necessary for a novice monk to know.

Among the most important of these compilations was the *Disputatio puerorum*. Composed in the early ninth century, the *Disputatio* consists of nine chapters on such diverse topics as the nature of the body and soul, the ordering of time, the books of the Old and New Testaments, the Mass, and the Lord's Prayer. Each chapter is composed of a series of questions and responses between a student and teacher, a format which enables its material to be arranged into short, manageable sections, often in enumerated lists easy to learn and memorize. The *Disputatio* survives in six manuscripts ranging from the ninth to the eleventh centuries, testifying to its continued use in the monasteries of the Carolingian and Holy Roman Empires. For those studying early medieval monastic culture, the *Disputatio* offers useful insight into the sort of training received by novices and oblates. Perhaps more importantly, the *Disputatio*'s dialogic structure sheds light on both the categories of knowledge considered valuable for beginning students and, in its sources, the range of texts upon which early monastic instruction was based. In a broader sense, it serves as an important witness to early medieval developments in Church doctrine and institutional practices, especially the evolution of the ecclesiastical grades and the reception of the Apostle's Creed.

Although the *Disputatio* has been printed twice before—first by Frobenius Forster in 1777, reprinted by J.P. Migne in the *Patrologia Latina* (101.1097–1144)—neither edition is easily available and both suffer from a number of serious shortcomings, including the erroneous attribution of the text to Alcuin of York. The goal of this new edition is to make available an authoritative, up-to-date and accessible version of the *Disputatio* in a format useful to researchers, teachers, and students alike. In so doing, it is hoped that the *Disputatio* will once again fulfill its original purpose as an instructional text while also serving as a valuable resource for the study of early monastic education.

The *Disputatio puerorum* and Carolingian Education

One of the constants of the Carolingian Renaissance, which continued after the death of Charlemagne into the ninth century, was the tension between the uniformity and organization of its educational program and the diverse ways in which that program came to be implemented. Charlemagne's vision for educational reform found expression in such texts as the legislative compilation *Admonitio generalis* (789) and the emperor's letter to Abbot Baugulf of Fulda, *Epistola de litteris colendis* (ca. 800). The *Admonitio* and *Epistola* both emphasize two foundational principles for the new Carolingian curriculum: first, students were to become fully literate in Latin, acquiring reading knowledge, a structural understanding of grammar and syntax, and spoken fluency; second, students were to engage in the systematic study of individual texts in an effort to both understand their relationship to Church doctrine and to ensure their preservation for future scholars.[3] Although Latin instruction remained relatively uniform across the empire, the texts that students went on to study differed from region to region and foundation to foundation. Glossaries such as the *Liber glossarum* and grammars such as Donatus' *Ars maior* (along with commentaries such as that of Sedulius Scottus on Donatus) were staples of virtually every Carolingian education, yet the material read afterwards varied considerably. One reason for this was the sheer number of works to be studied, ranging from Augustine and Jerome to Isidore of Seville and Bede, the scope of which made it impossible for every student to be taught every text, let alone all of the information these works contained. The problem was particularly acute in the

3 For the *Admonitio generalis* and the *Epistola de litteris colendis*, see Alfred Boretius, *Capitularia regum Francorum: tomus primus, legum sectio II*, Monumenta Germaniae Historica (Hannover, 1883), 52–62 and 79. The relevant passages occur on pp. 59 (line 42)–60 (line 7) and p. 79 (lines 37–42). An entire library of scholarship exists on the Carolingian educational program, but a useful overview can be found in John Contreni, 'The Carolingian Renaissance: Education and Literary Culture,' in *The New Cambridge Medieval History* vol. 1: *c. 700–c. 900*, ed. Rosamond McKitterick (Cambridge, 1995), 709–775.

case of Isidore's *Etymologiae*, the sheer breadth of which—twenty books encompassing virtually every aspect of contemporary knowledge—made it inaccessible to all but the most gifted students.

One common solution to this problem was the composition of abbreviated compilations such as the *Disputatio*: easily accessible texts in dialogic format adaptable for a variety of potential uses.[4] Students in cathedral schools utilized such texts to grasp the rudiments of religious knowledge, learning such concepts in order to become teachers themselves. Likewise, laymen studied the same material to fulfill Charlemagne's demand that each of his subjects acquire a basic understanding of the Mass, the Lord's Prayer and the Creed.[5] Indeed, even adult converts from conquered lands could learn the catechetical information necessary to be baptized and enter into the Christian faith. In reframing the major texts of Church doctrine as short dialogues, compilations such as the *Disputatio* translated complex theological concepts into a form more easily understood by beginning students. The use of a dialogic format reflects the structure of the grammatical treatises with which the students would already have been familiar. As Martin Irvine has observed in his studies of early medieval grammatical education,

> … the grammatical discipline was not simply descriptive […] but productive of knowledge: it supplied a network of presuppositions, discursive strategies, and rules for argumentation that governed inquiry and provided the grounds of possibility for knowledge. Grammar was thus a paradigm […] and a discursive practice that supplied the conditions for knowledge.[6]

In other words, the question-and-answer format that made grammatical knowledge so much easier to learn was then ap-

4 See Alex J. Novikoff, *The Medieval Culture of Disputation: Pedagogy, Practice, and Performance* (Philadelphia, 2013), 8–33.

5 See the stipulations of the Synod of Frankfurt (794) §33, 50, and 53. On this point, see Anne C. McGuire, 'Liturgy and the Laity in the Ninth Century,' *Ecclesia Orans* 13 (1996) 463–494.

6 Martin Irvine, *The Making of Textual Culture: 'Grammatica' and Literary Theory, 350–1100* (Cambridge, 1994), 8.

plied towards the explication and creation of other educational texts, so that students could more easily digest difficult theological concepts in a manner that they had already experienced.

The success of the *Disputatio puerorum* as an instructional text is indicated by its attestation in manuscripts copied over a 200 year period with provenances ranging from southeast Germany to northern France. Extended passages from the *Disputatio* occur in the writings of Bishop Bruno of Würzburg (ca. 1005–1045) as well as the English Pontifical of St. Dunstan and the Lanalet Pontifical. Its influence can also be found in a series of later ordinals preserved in Barcelona, Vich Museo Episcopal 39; Cambridge, Corpus Christi College 44; and Dublin, Trinity College Lat. 218.[7] The reuse of material from the *Disputatio* testifies to its importance to the Carolingian educational program. By virtue of the flexibility that allowed it to serve multiple purposes, the *Disputatio puerorum* could appeal to a broader readership than could a more traditional encyclopedic text such as Isidore's *Etymologiae*. While Isidore was concerned with the passage of all knowledge down to future generations, compiling information about everything known in the universe at the time, ninth-century scholars were more concerned with how various elements of knowledge could best be presented to students. By adapting the question-and-answer format of grammatical texts for use in teaching theological concepts, the author of the *Disputatio puerorum* distilled the knowledge of his sources and reshaped it into something much more suited to the classroom.

Manuscripts

The six extant manuscripts containing all or part of the *Disputatio* are:

A Vienna, Österreichische Nationalbibliothek, 458 (Salzburg, s ix^{med})

7 On Bruno of Würzburg, see *PL* 142:39–568, especially 559–561. See also n. to VIII.1 below. On the *Disputatio*'s influence on later pontifical and ordinals, see Roger E. Reynolds, *The Ordinals of Christ from Their Origins to the Twelfth Century* (Berlin, 1978), 79–80.

B Vienna, Österreichische Nationalbibliothek, 966 (St. Emmeram, s ix^{med})

C Munich, Bayerische Staatsbibliothek, Clm 5257 (Chiemsee, s xi)

D Munich, Bayerische Staatsbibliothek, Clm 14510 (St. Emmeram, s ix$^{2/4}$)

E St. Petersburg, Publichnaja Biblioteka, O.v.I.7 (Northern France? s ix^{med})

F Toronto, University of Toronto, MS 45, fragment 24–5 (St. Emmeram, s ix$^{2/4}$)

The *Disputatio* occurs complete in only two of these manuscripts (MSS A and C); B runs through VIII.23; D to II.108; E is only a fragment comprising IX.3–15; and F is a fragment corresponding to questions VIII.1–13. A pattern of shared errors and omissions suggests that each of the MSS derives from an original manuscript [a], however MSS B, C, and D share an additional set of variants, suggesting that they derive from a lost exemplar, [b]. Some examples of these variants include the substitution of *praecellit* for *praecedit* at II.14, the substitution of *aspectet* for *exspectet* at II.19, the substitution of *sicut eximius* for *quasi eximius* at II.89, and the awkward blending of quotations from Isidore and Sedulius at IV.52 (see note). Taken together, the scribal variants indicate the following stemma (omitting the fragments E and F, the brevity of which makes it impossible to determine a genealogy):

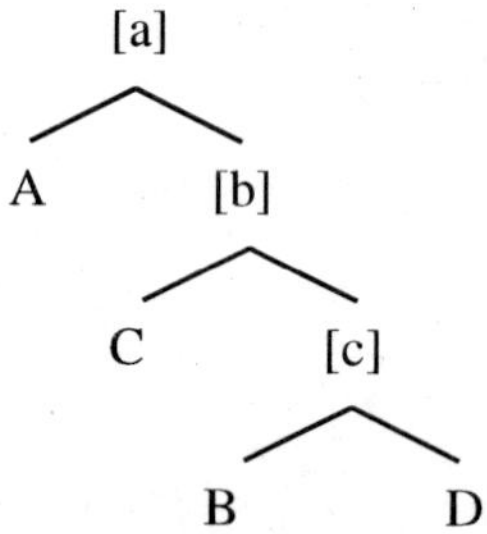

As this stemma indicates, of the two complete texts of the *Disputatio*, MS A is the one that appears to approximate most closely the *Urtext* [a]. It is this recension of the *Disputatio* that is edited in this volume.

MS A has been dated by Bischoff to the mid-ninth century, and bears the colophon of the *magister* Baldo, [8] who supervised the Salzburg scriptorium during the bishoprics of Adalram (821–836) and Liuphram (836–859). The manuscript consists of 191 folia with dimensions of 282×188 mm. and a textblock of approximately 208×128 mm. The folia are numbered in the upper right-hand corner of the recto with 61 inadvertently being used twice.[9] The hand is a neat Caroline miniscule. The manuscript was compiled in two separate phases, the first of which produced the copy of Adamnan's *De locis sanctis Jerusalem,* an account of Bishop Arculf's travels to Jerusalem in the year 680. In Bischoff's opinion, this text is written in a much lighter hand than that of the rest of the manuscript, and was most likely written at an earlier time, during the bishopric of Adalram. The rest of the manuscript was then written later, during Liuphram's bishopric, as evidenced by a much heavier hand that is usually found in manuscripts dating from that period, as well as by the boundaries of the text, which extend further out into the margins than the earlier section.

The contents of the manuscript are as follows:
fols. 1r–26v: Adamnan, *De locis sanctis Jerusalem.*
fols. 27r–81r: *Disputatio puerorum.*

8 The colophon reads: 'Hunc humilis librum fecit perscribere Baldo/ reddat in aeternum mitis cui praemia Christus.' For a full account of the manuscript, see Bernhard Bischoff, *Die südostdeutschen Schreibschulen und Bibliotheken in der Karolingerzeit, II: Die vorwiegend österreichischen Diözesen* (Wiesbaden, 1980), 78, 82, 83, 155f. This manuscript is also sigla X in Dümmler's edition of Alcuin's letters: Philipp Jaffé, Ernst Dümmler, and Wilhelm Wattenbach, *Bibliotheca rerum Germanicarum,* vol. 6: Monumenta Alcuiniana (Aalen, 1964), 138. For further description, also see Wilhelm Levison, 'Die älteste Lebensbeschreibung Ruperts von Salzburg,' *Neues Archiv für ältere deutsche Geschichtskunde* 28 (1902–1903) 292–294; Reynolds, *The Ordinals of Christ from Their Origins to the Twelfth Century,* 79; Reynolds, 'Canon Law Collections in Early Ninth-Century Salzburg,' in *Proceedings of the Fifth International Congress of Medieval Canon Law: Salamanca, 21–25 September 1976,* ed. Stephan Kuttner and Kenneth Pennington (Città del Vaticano, 1980), 32.

9 See below, p. 69.

fols. 81v–86v: Alcuin, *Epistola ad Arnonem.*[10]
fols. 86v–114r: Alcuin, *Expositio in psalmos poenitentialis.*
fols. 114r–143r: Alcuin, *Expositio in psalmum cxviii.*
fols. 143r–168r: Alcuin, *Expositio in psalmos graduales.*[11]
fols. 168r–175r: Alcuin, *Epistola ad pueros S. Martini de confessione puerorum.*[12]
fols. 175r–179r: *Dicta Albini de imagine dei.*[13]
fols. 179r–186r: Paulinus of Aquileia, *Dictatus de baptismate.*[14]
fols. 186r–189v: Alcuin, *Dictatus seu Epistola ad Karolum Magnum.*[15]
fols. 189v–191v: *Concio de honestate et religione conservanda.*[16]

Sources

In organizing his material, the author of the *Disputatio* drew on an extensive list of sources, the range of which suggests that he had a well-stocked monastic library easily available. Reflecting the text's pedagogical function, the *Disputatio* author relied most on the writings of the post-Nicene Church fathers. Of these, the most significant was Isidore of Seville, three of whose works—the *Etymologiae*, *De ecclesiasticis officiis*, and *In libros veteris ac novi testamenti Prooemia*—provide direct or indirect source material for more than 200 question/answer sets, accounting for almost half of the *Disputatio* as a whole. By far the most influential of Isidore's works was the *Etymolo-*

10 This letter is from Alcuin to Arno, and serves as a preface to the psalm expositions.
11 These three psalm expositions are found in *PL* 100:569–638.
12 *PL* 101:649–656.
13 *PL* 100:565–568.
14 This text was perhaps written following his participation in the Salzburg synod of 796, where the evangelization and baptism of the barbarians were of primary concern.
15 *PL* 100:565–568. Also entitled *De ordinandis piis praedicatoribus*, this text is a letter from Alcuin to Charlemagne containing instructions on how the newly conquered barbarian Huns should best be converted to faith in Christ.
16 A fragment of an anonymous sermon.

giae, which alone served as the source for 140 question/answer sets. The near omnipresence of the Middle Ages' greatest encyclopedist reflects the similarly encyclopedic aspirations behind the *Disputatio*'s composition. As a text designed to communicate basic Christian doctrine involving the physical world, the spiritual world, the Bible, and the liturgy, the *Disputatio* shared the same impulse towards comprehensiveness that stood behind the *Etymologiae*, but for a more inexperienced reader.

This need to communicate the fundamentals of Church theology also informed the *Disputatio*'s use of such other patristic writers as Augustine and Pope Gregory I, though their footprint on the text is far smaller than Isidore's. Material from Augustine's *De Genesi contra Manicheos* can be found in I.3, and Gregory's *Dialogues* serve as the source for II.74–76, yet here citations from their work end. Saint Jerome's writings are nowhere quoted directly in the text (other than his Latin Bible, of course), yet II.89–108 are based on a section of the *Etymologiae* which Isidore describes as a borrowing from Jerome's *De decem nominibus dei*. More allusively, Jerome's continuation of Eusebius' *Chronicon* is mentioned in III.4, while the Latin rendering of Ecclesiastes 1:6 in II.84, is one found in several of Jerome's commentaries, though it appears in other texts known to the *Disputatio* author as well. Finally, perhaps the most obscure of the *Disputatio*'s patristic sources is the anonymous fourth-century tract *De traditione symboli*, believed in the early Middle Ages to be the work of Bishop Maximus of Turin, which serves as the principal source for VIII.21–36.

The author of the *Disputatio* also drew on more contemporary sources, particularly English and Irish texts of the seventh and eighth centuries popular among members of the Carolingian court school. Not surprisingly, texts associated with Bede and Alcuin are particularly influential. For instance, the account of the creation in I.4 is taken directly from Bede's *De natura rerum*, while Bede's *De temporibus* furnishes material for the detailed account of the periodization of history in III.1. In the case of Alcuin, the *Disputatio* quotes his *De orthographia* in IV.37. More tenuously, the *Dicta Albini de imagine dei*, a text

wrongly attributed to Alcuin, provides the source for II.2–13. The Irish sources for the *Disputatio* are more eclectic and, to the modern reader, more obscure, however they include texts which strongly influenced later Carolingian thought, most notably the pseudo-Isidorian *Quaestiones tam de nouo quam de uetere testamentum* [*sic*], the *Liber de numeris*, and the *Prebiarum de multorum exemplaribus*, and several Hiberno-Gallican ordinals of Christ.[17] More well-known is the *Carmen Paschale* of Sedulius Scottus, which the *Disputatio* quotes in IV.52.

Authorship

Among the most significant problems confronting the reader of the *Disputatio puerorum* is the identity of its author. Traditionally, the *Disputatio* has been ascribed to Alcuin of York (ca. 735–804), abbot of Tours and a leading member of the scholarly circle that emerged under the patronage of the Emperor Charlemagne; however much about the text and its provenance suggests that the *Disputatio* may come from the pen of someone writing in a context far removed from the monastic library at Tours, suggesting that we should be wary of claiming Alcuin's authorship too definitively.

The attribution of the *Disputatio* to Alcuin originates with its first editor, Frobenius Forster, *abbas princeps* of St. Emmeram in Regensburg, who included it (along with a number of other dubious texts) in his 1777 collected edition of Alcuin's works. Migne incorporated Forster's edition into the *Patrologia Latina* (*PL*101:1097–1144), and likewise accepted the latter's attribution. Forster outlined three reasons suggesting Alcuin's authorship: first, three of the manuscripts in which the *Disputatio* is preserved (MSS A, B, and D) also contain works attributable to

17 The *Quaestiones* is a *florilegium* in dialogic form concerning, as the title suggests, the Old and New Testaments. The *Liber de Numeris* is likewise a *florilegium*, this time organized by numerical subjects (the five senses, etc.). The *Prebiarum* (likely a corruption of *breviarium*) is an instructional dialogue similar to the *Disputatio*. The so-called 'ordinals of Christ' were compilations of Scripural passages designed to characterize the different Church offices as imitative of Christ's biography.

Alcuin;[18] second, according to Forster the style and method of the *Disputatio* are 'similar to the style and method of Alcuin, as an egg to an egg';[19] and finally, the text includes passages taken from of a tract known as the *Dicta beati Albini levitae super illud Geneseos* (*Dicta Albini*), incorrectly supposed by Forster to have been authored by Alcuin. According to Forster, if it could be proved decisively that Alcuin was the author of the *Dicta Albini*, it would count as compelling evidence for his authorship of the *Disputatio*.

Forster's arguments cannot be considered conclusive, though. The stylistic argument is particularly weak: because the *Disputatio* largely consists of lightly adapted excerpts from the works of other authors, it lacks the sort of distinctive, standalone passages in which identifiable features of Alcuin's prose might be found. Insofar as a text of this sort might be described as having a 'style,' it is that of Isidore of Seville, Bede, Pseudo-Maximus, and Gregory the Great— all authors whose works were mined for the composition for the *Disputatio*. Although it is possible that the text was assembled by Alcuin, little in the prose suggests as much. Equally significant is the absence of a manuscript tradition linking Alcuin's name to the text. For nearly all of his authentic works, Alcuin attached some kind of dedicatory epistle or preface (as did Bede and such contemporaries of Alcuin's as Claudius of Turin and Rabanus Maurus). In MS A, Alcuin's letter to Arno also serves as the preface to the expositions on the penitential and gradual psalms. In MS D, Alcuin's *De fide sanctae trinitatis* is headed by another letter, this one from Alcuin to Charlemagne, which acts as a preface and an acknowledgment of Alcuin's authorship. Likewise, Alcuin's *Dialogus de rhetorica et virtutibus* contains a short verse poem, provides an introduction, and names the interlocutors (Charlemagne and Alcuin); while Alcuin's preface to his *Vita sancti Willibrordi* records that he composed the work during his few free moments

18 MS A includes two letters by Alcuin and three of his Biblical commentaries, MS B includes two of Alcuin's letters, and MS D. contains Alcuin's *De fide sanctae trinitatis*.

19 *PL* 101:1099: 'secundo stylus et methodus hujus tractatus stylo ac methodo Alcuini ita similes sunt, ut ovum ovo [...].'

at night. In all, of the seventeen clearly authentic Alcuinian texts fifteen carry some form of dedicatory preface.[20] In the words of Michael Gorman, then, 'it is clear that the prefaces to [Alcuin's] works were closely linked to his letter writing activity.'[21] As such, even as Alcuin's surviving prefatory letters testify to the parameters of his corpus, the absence of any similar preface attached to or referencing the *Disputatio* suggests that claims concerning his authorship should be viewed with some suspicion.

Also suggestive is a short passage unique to MS A indicating that the *Disputatio* ought to be attributed to someone other than Alcuin. The passage in question, IV.37, reads,

> **37.** IN. Cur dicitur 'hodie'?
> RESP. 'Hodie,' quasi 'hoc die,' sic et 'quottidie,' non 'cotidie,' ut sit quot diebus. Alicubi aliter legitur, 'non a quota die, sed a continenti die "cotidie" dicitur.'

The quotation at the end of the response is omitted from every other manuscript witness of the *Disputatio*. While the rest of the response derives from Isidore's *Etymologiae*, the quotation comes from Alcuin's *De orthographia*. While this latter is, in turn, adapted largely from Bede's orthographic treatise of the same name, the sentence 'non a quota...dicitur' does not occur in Bede and appears to be original to Alcuin's work. If this is the case, it seems unlikely that Alcuin, were he the author of the *Disputatio*, would preface the quotation with the phrase

20 Michael Gorman, 'Alcuin before Migne,' *Revue Bénédictine* 112 (2002) 101–102. The two that do not have these prefaces are the *Contra haeresim Felicis* and the *De dialectica*. However, Gorman may go a little too far when he says that anything else that does not have a preface could not have been written by Alcuin. For example, he discounts Alcuin as the author of the *Disputatio Pippini cum Albino*, saying that 'it is difficult to imagine that this drivel...from various banal sources such as the *Ioca monachorum* was put together by Alcuin' (128). But the *Disputatio Pippini* is much more than drivel, and is an intriguing example of Alcuin's format of the question-and-answer dialogue, which also displays the kind of hierarchy and order that is the norm in the Carolingian world. Since Gorman does admit that the question of authorship remains open on other dubious texts, perhaps this one, too, should be included in that category.

21 Gorman, 'Alcuin Before Migne,' 102.

'alicubi aliter legitur.' A similar, though somewhat weaker, claim can also be made concerning II.2, in which a quotation from the *Dicta Albini de imagine dei* is preceded by the phrase, 'Secundum quod legi, faciam quod petisti.' Although the arguments for Alcuin's authorship of the *Dicta Albini* are considered dubious at best, Forster argues that this borrowing supports Alcuin's authorship of the *Disputatio*; however, if we accept Forster's claim that Alcuin composed the *Dicta Albini*, it again seems unlikely that he would refer to his own work as simply something 'quod legi.'

Finally, the range of patristic and insular sources available to the author as well as the distribution of surviving manuscripts point to an eastern Carolingian provenance, far from the Palace School in Aachen or Alcuin's abbey at Tours. The wide variety of sources available to the author of the *Disputatio* indicates that it must have been compiled at one of the relatively few foundations with a library large enough to include such a diverse group of texts. The most likely candidates are St. Peter's Abbey of Salzburg and St. Emmeram's Abbey of Regensburg. While patristic texts can be found at a number of houses throughout Carolingian Francia, the influence of the Irish-born Bishop Vergilius of Salzburg (ca. 700–784) meant that these foundations, the former especially, boasted significant insular collections as well. Indeed, texts similar to the *Disputatio* in dialogic structure and range of source material can be traced to the scriptoria of both houses.[22] Taking into account the fact that four of the six extant manuscripts survive from St. Peter's or St. Emmeram's (and a fifth was compiled at nearby Chiemsee), it seems logical to date and locate the *Disputatio*'s composition

22 Bernhard Bischoff, *Die südostdeutschen Schreibschulen*, vol. 1 (1940), 229–232; Robert McNally, *Scriptores Hiberniae Minores, Pars I*, Corpus Christianorum Series Latina, vol. 108B (Turnhout, 1973), 155–159; Reynolds, 'Canon Law Collections,' 16, 28–29; Charles D. Wright, *The Irish Tradition in Old English Literature*, ed. Simon Keynes and Michael Lapidge, Cambridge Studies in Anglo-Saxon England, vol. 6 (Cambridge, 1993), 49–105; John Marenbon, *From the Circle of Alcuin to the School of Auxerre: Logic, Theology, and Philosophy in the Early Middle Ages*, Cambridge Studies in Medieval Life and Thought, 3rd ser., vol. 15 (Cambridge, 1981), 30–43, 144–151.

to the early ninth century in the Regensburg-Salzburg region of Southeast Germany.

Taken together, the case against Alcuin's authorship is not strong enough to rule out his involvement in the *Disputatio*'s composition entirely, yet it does raise serious doubts. Most of the other works Forster identified as Alcuinian have since been rejected, while the arguments he mustered are unsupported—and in some instances, contradicted—by the text itself. Moreover, the likelihood that the text was composed in Regensburg or Salzburg, both far from Alcuin's diocese of Tours, indicates an origin in the eastern rather than the western empire. In brief, then, it is the conclusion of the editors that the authorship of the *Disputatio* must remain an open question.

Notes to the Edition

The following edition is based on the A-recension of the *Disputatio*, Vienna, Österreichische Nationalbibliothek, 458. Where appropriate, minor emendations following the sources consulted by the *Disputatio*'s author have been incorporated to clarify the text for student readers. In such cases the manuscript readings are always included in the apparatus criticus. In rare instances, scribal error or omission has made it necessary to supply text from other manuscripts. These passages have been marked with angular brackets. Square brackets identify words present in the manuscript, but which may indicate scribal error and ought to be excised.

The capitalization and punctuation are both editorial. In matters of orthography, we have reproduced the spellings which appear in MS A without regularization; however, abbreviations, hybrid numerical appreviations (i.e. 'iiii-or' for 'quattuor'), and instances of *e caudata* have been silently expanded. Numbers have also been inserted into the text to aid in the citation of individual question/answer sets.

The commentary below the text identifies major sources for specific lines of the text and clarifies aspects that might require explanation. The apparatus criticus below the commentary lists significant variants from other manuscripts and notes some non-standard spellings to help the student reader of the edition.

Finally, the metawords in the text pose a special problem. The manuscript does not distinguish them from the main text, but this can cause considerable confusion for student readers. In order to make the text more accessible, our principle has been to enclose metawords in quotation marks in those cases in which the text refers to a lexeme and in which the answer involves a discussion of etymology. We have omitted quotation marks in those cases in which the text refers to a concept and the answer involves a discussion of theology rather than language. In practice however, this distinction doesn't always hold up as these two categories of explanation often overlap. Inevitably, inconsistencies occur and, in such cases, we have tried to err on the side of omission rather than inclusion.

MANUSCRIPT SIGLA

A Vienna, Österreichische Nationalbibliothek, 458 (Salzburg, s ix^{med})

B Vienna, Österreichische Nationalbibliothek, 966 (St. Emmeram, s ix^{med})

C Munich, Bayerische Staatsbibliothek, Clm 5257 (Chiemsee, s xi)

D Munich, Bayerische Staatsbibliothek, Clm 14510 (St. Emmeram, s ix$^{2/4}$)

E St. Petersburg, Publichnaja Biblioteka, O.v.I.7 (Northern France? s ix^{med})

F Toronto, University of Toronto, MS 45, fragment 24–5 (St. Emmeram, s ix$^{2/4}$)

SELECTED BIBLIOGRAPHY

Bischoff, Bernhard. *Die südostdeutschen Schreibschulen und Bibliotheken in der Karolingerzeit*, 2 vols. (Wiesbaden, 1940, 1980).

Boretius, Alfred, ed. *Capitularia regum Francorum: tomus primus, legum sectio II*. Monumenta Germaniae Historica (Hannover, 1883).

Contreni, John. 'The Carolingian Renaissance: Education and Literary Culture.' In *The New Cambridge Medieval History* vol. 1: *c. 700–c. 900*, ed. Rosamond McKitterick (Cambridge, 1995) 709–757.

de Vogüé, Adalbert, ed. *Gregory the Great: Dialogorum libri quatuor de miraculis patrum Italicorum*. Sources Chrétiennes. 3 vols (Paris, 1978–1980).

Irvine, Martin. *The Making of Textual Culture: 'Grammatica' and Literary Theory, 350–1100* (Cambridge, 1994).

Gorman, Michael. 'Alcuin before Migne.' *Revue Bénédictine* 112 (2002) 101–130.

Jaffé, Philipp, Ernst Dümmler, and Wilhelm Wattenbach, eds. *Bibliotheca rerum Germanicarum*, vol. 6: Monumenta Alcuiniana (Aalen, 1964).

Jones, Christopher W., ed. *Bedae Venerabilis Opera: Pars I, Opera didascalia*. Corpus Christianorum Series Latina, vol. 123B (Turnhout, 1977).

Leclerq, Jean. *The Love of Learning and the Desire for God: A Study of Monastic Culture* (New York, 1961).

Lindsay, W.M., ed. *Isidori Hispalensis episcopi Etymologiarum sive originum libri XX*, 2 vols (Oxford, 1911).

Marenbon, John. *From the Circle of Alcuin to the School of Auxerre: Logic, Theology, and Philosophy in the Early Middle Ages*. Cambridge Studies in Medieval Life and Thought, 3rd ser., vol. 15 (Cambridge, 1981).

Matter, E. Ann. 'Alcuin's Question-and-Answer Texts.' *Rivista di Storia della Filosofia* 45.4 (1990) 645–656.

McGuire, Anne C. 'Liturgy and the Laity in the Ninth Century.' *Ecclesia Orans* 13 (1996) 463–494.

McNally, Robert, ed. *Scriptores Hiberniae minores, Pars I.* Corpus Christianorum Series Latina, vol. 108B (Turnhout, 1973).

Migne, Jacques-Paul, ed. *Disputatio puerorum.* Patrologia Latina 101:1097–1114 (repr. of 1st ed. by Frobenius, 1777).

Novikoff, Alex J. *The Medieval Culture of Disputation: Pedagogy, Practice, and Performance* (Philadelphia, 2013).

Pfaff, Richard W. *The Liturgy in Medieval England* (Cambridge, 2009).

Rabin, Andrew. 'Historical Re-Collections: Rewriting the World Chronicle in Bede's *De Temporum Ratione.*' *Viator* 36 (2005) 23–39.

Reynolds, L.D., ed. *Texts and Transmission: A Survey of the Latin Classics* (Oxford, 1984).

Reynolds, Roger E. 'Canon Law Collections in Early Ninth-Century Salzburg.' In *Proceedings of the Fifth International Congress of Medieval Canon Law: Salamanca, 21–25 September 1976*, ed. Stephan Kuttner and Kenneth Pennington (Città del Vaticano, 1980) 15–34.

—. *The Ordinals of Christ from Their Origins to the Twelfth Century* (Berlin, 1978).

Riché, Pierre. *Education and Culture in the Barbarian West from the Sixth through the Eighth Centuries*, trans. John Contreni (Columbia, 1976).

Wright, Charles D. *The Irish Tradition in Old English Literature.* Cambridge Studies in Anglo-Saxon England, vol. 6 (Cambridge, 1993).

Disputatio puerorum

A Ninth-Century Monastic Instructional Text

Edited from
Vienna,
Österreichische Nationalbibliothek,
458

IN NOMINE DIVINO TRINO INCIPIT SENTENTIA PRIMA DE OPERIBVS SEX DIERVM IVXTA DISPVTATIONEM PVERORVM CVM INTERROGATIONIBVS ET RESPONSIONIBVS EIVS 27r

1. IN. Et quia humana fragilitas nec audet nec potest aliunde exordium sumere rationis, nisi a principio operis Conditoris, idcirco si uestrae dominationi audire placuerit, in quantum eo largiente qui cuncta creauit conceditur, uolumus de distinctionibus sex dierum operum in praesentia uestra aliquid rationis deducere.

RESP. Eia condiscipule, quoniam sicut dixi et ipse nosti, nec possumus nec audemus altius initium nostrae protrahere disputationis. Si tibi uidetur incipiamus ab eodem principio, et prout Dominus donare dignatur, disputemus de distinctionibus praefatarum sex dierum suorumque operum.

<I> DE OPERIBVS SEX DIERVM

1. <IN.> Nequaquam disputationem nostram aliubi melius incipere posse arbitror, quam / ab ipsa prima creatione et a 27v
praescripto sacrato et perfecto numero, sicut adseruisti, qui ex omni parte perfectus est. Iam quia ita iudicasti, fiat ita. Sed primum peto, ut dicas, quomodo perfectus esse constet?

RESP. Ideo enim perfectus esse dicitur, quia partibus suis completur.

2. IN. Qua ratione?

RESP. Habet quippe unum, quod est sexta pars eius; duo, quod est tertia; tres, quod est medium; unum ergo, duo, et tres sex faciunt, cuius perfectio ita completa est.

3. IN. Quoniam ab illo principio incipiendam disputationem

13 *Si*: the scribe treats this as the beginning of a separate *interrogatio*, but both the syntax and the placement of the rubric suggest this to be an error.

25–27 *Habet…est*: For parallels to this passage, see *Liber numerorum* VII (*PL* 83:184). See also the *Liber de divinis officiis*, Caput X: 'Nam senarius numerus perfectus est, et suis cȯmpletur particus. Est enim sexta pars eius, unum; secunda, tria; tertia vero, duo. Unum ergo et duo et tria, fiunt sex.' (*PL* 101:1188).

28–38 This question and response closely parallels the *De Genesi contra*

16 *Capitals appear in the manuscript.* **17** <IN>: RESP. *MS*

nostram esse censuisti, dic mihi in quo principio ipsam creationem condidisset omnipotens Deus; in principio temporis an in principio Verbi Dei, quod est unigenitus Filius Dei?
RESP. Non in principio temporis, sed in principio Verbi Dei, de quo et beatus Iohannes euangelista ait: *In principio erat Verbum, et Verbum erat apud Deum, et Deus erat Verbum; omnia per ipsum facta sunt, et sine ipso factum est nihil.* Vnde et ipse Dominus in Euangelio interrogantibus: *Tu quis es?* Respondit: *Ego initium, qui et loquor uobis.* In hoc ergo principio fecit omnipotens Deus caelum et terram, mare, et omnia quae in eis sunt. / 28r

4. IN. Nunc uolo ut omnes distinctiones singulorum operum supradictorum dierum per ordinem mihi exponas.
RESP. Primo die lux ex nihilo facta est; secundo, firmamentum in medio aquarum; tertio, species maris et terrae cum his, quae terrae radicitus inhaerent; quarto, luminaria caeli de lumine primo die facto; quinto, natalia et uolatilia de aquis; sexto, uero reliqua animalia de terra; et homo carne quidem de terra, anima autem de nihilo constat, de quo, cum creandus esset, Deus ait: *Faciamus hominem ad imaginem et similitudinem nostram.*

<II> DE NATVRA HOMINIS

1. IN. Quoniam creator omnium ad imaginem et similitudinem suam hominem creare dignatus est, inquiramus dili

---

Manicheos of Augustine of Hippo: 'Et quid ei subito placuit facere, quod nunquam antea fecerat per tempora aeterna? Hic respondemus, deum in principio fecisse coelum et terram, non in principio temporis, sed in Christo, cum verbum esset apud patrem, per quod facta et in quo facta sunt omnia.' (1.2.3, *PL* 34:173–220)

33–35 *In...nihil*: Io 1:1, 3

36–37 *Tu...uobis*: Io 8:25

39–47 This question and response derives from Bede, *De natura rerum*, Caput II: 'Die autem primo lux facta est, et ipsa de nihilo; secundo, firmamentum in medio aquarum; tertio, species maris et terrae, cum eis quae terrae radicitus inhaerent; quarto, luminaria coeli de lumine primo die facto; quinto, natatilia et volatilia de aquis; sexto, reliqua animalia de terra, et homo quidem carne de terra, anima vero de nihilo creatus.' Edited in Christopher W. Jones, *Bedae venerabilis opera: pars I, opera didascalia*. Corpus Christianorum Series Latina, vol. 123A (Turnhout, 1977), 192–234.

47 *Faciamus...nostram*: Gen 1:26

genter, quomodo aut qualiter ad imaginem eius homo creatus esse dicatur?

RESP. Faciamus ut dicis, eo quod necesse est nobis scire, in quantum ab eo conceditur, qualiter ab ipso creati sumus, ut eius misericordiam magis laudare ualeamus, quia, ut ita dicam, si omnia membra nostra in linguas conuerti potuissent, nullatenus pro sola creatione, qua nos creare dignatus est, dignas ei laudes referre ualuissemus. / 28v

2. IN. Consentio per omnia, ut dicis, sed peto humiliter, ut quomodo uel qualiter ab eo creati esse fateamur, quantum ex te est, mihi indicare non rennuas.

RESP. Secundum quod legi, faciam quod petisti. Tanta dignitas humanae conditionis esse cognoscitur, ut non solo iubentis sermone, sicut alia sex dierum opera, sed consilio sanctae Trinitatis et opere diuinae maiestatis creatus est homo, in quo ait: *Faciamus hominem ad imaginem et similitudinem nostram*, quod ideo ei praestitit conditor, ut tanto ardentius eum amaret, quanto se mirabilius ab eo esse conditum intellegeret, et ne hoc solum ei concessit, quod consilio sanctae Trinitatis sic eum condidit, sed etiam quod ad imaginem et similitudinem suam eum creauit, quod nulli alii ex creaturis donauit.

3. IN. Verum est, ut asseris, sed quomodo ad imaginem suam eum creasset, ut mihi aperias obsecro.

RESP. Primo quidem ad imaginem suam eum creauit, quod in nobilitate interioris hominis considerare debemus, ut sicuti Deus unus semper ubique totus est, omnia uiuificans, mouens, / 29r
et gubernans, sicut Apostolus confirmat, quod *in eo uiuimus, mouemur, et sumus*, sic anima in suo corpore ubique tota uiget, uiuificans eum, mouens, et gubernans.

59–161 Questions 2 through 13 are based on the *Dicta Albini de imagine dei*, ed. in John Marenbon, *From the Circle of Alcuin to the School of Auxerre: Logic, Theology, and Philosophy in the Early Middle Ages*, Cambridge Studies in Medieval Life and Thought, 3rd ser., vol. 15 (Cambridge, 1981), 158–161. In keeping with his practice throughout the rest of the *Disputatio*, the author has converted his source into dialogic form.

66 *Faciamus…nostram*: Gen 1:26

77–78 *in eo…sumus*: Act 17:28

71 alii: alio *MS*

4. IN. Dic mihi, si eadem anima, quam interiorem hominem esse dixisti, in quibusdam maioribus membris corporis sui sit maior et in minoribus minor? Aut etiam si singularem locum in eodem corpore teneat, an non?

RESP. Nec locum ibi singularem obtinet, nec in maioribus membris maior et in minoribus minor, sed in minimis tota et in maximis tota; et haec est imago unitatis omnipotentis Dei, quam anima habet in se.

5. IN. Potest eadem anima aliquam Trinitatis habere imaginem, an non?

RESP. Vtique potest.

6. IN. Quomodo?

RESP. Primo enim quia sicut Deus est, uiuit, et sapit, ita anima secundum suum modum est, uiuit, et sapit.

7. IN. Potest in hoc aliam habere rationem?

RESP. Potest.

8. IN. Quomodo?

RESP. Est enim alia trinitas in ea, qua ad imaginem sui conditoris, perfectae quidem et summae Trinitatis, quae est in Patre et Filio et Spiritu Sancto, condita, quae licet unius sit naturae, tres / tamen in se dignitates habet. 29v

9. IN. Quae sunt hae?

RESP. Id est intellectum, uoluntatem, et memoriam. Vnde et Dominus in Euangelio: *Diliges Dominum Deum tuum ex toto corde tuo et ex tota anima tua et ex tota mente tua, id est ex toto intellectu et ex tota uoluntate et ex tota memoria.*

10. IN. Qua ratione haec sibi conueniunt?

RESP. Quia sicut ex Patre generatur Filius, ex Patre Filioque procedit Spiritus Sanctus, ita ex intellectu generatur uoluntas, et ex his item ambobus procedit memoria. Et hoc facile intellegi potest, quia sine his tribus perfecta anima esse non potest; nec horum trium unum aliquod, quantum ad suam pertinet beatitudinem, sine aliis duobus integrum constat.

11. IN. Adhuc de eadem re a te audire desidero.

RESP. Et ego tibi prout scio adhuc dicam. Sicut enim Deus Pater, Deus Filius, Deus Spiritus Sanctus est, non tamen tres dii sunt, sed unus Deus tres habens personas, ita anima intellectus,

103–105 *Diliges…memoria*: Mt 22:37, Mc 12:30, Lc 10:27

anima uoluntas, anima memoria; non tamen tres animae in uno corpore, sed una anima tres habens dignitates, atque in his tribus eius imaginem mirabiliter gerit in sua natura noster interior homo, ex / quibus quasi excellentioribus animae dignitatibus 30r
iubemur diligere conditorem, ut quantum intellegatur diligatur, et quantum diligatur semper in memoria habeatur. Nec solus sufficit de eo intellectus, nisi fiat in amore eius uoluntas; nec etiam haec duo sufficiunt, nisi memoria addatur, qua semper in mente intellegentis et diligentis maneat Deus. Et sicut nullum potest esse momentum, quo homo non utatur uel fruatur Dei bonitate et misericordia, ita nullum debeat esse momentum, quo praesentem eum non habeat memoria.

12. IN. Haec de imagine hac uice mihi sufficiunt; sed qualiter ad similitudinem Dei creati sumus, innotesce.

RESP. In quantum ipso conditore largiente ualeo, faciam. Sicut enim Deus creator, qui nos ad similitudinem suam creauit, est caritas, est bonus, iustus et patiens, mitis et mundus, atque misericors, et cetera uirtutum sanctarum insignia, quae de eo leguntur, ita homo creatus est, ut caritatem haberet, ut bonus esset et iustus, ut patiens atque mitis, mundus et misericors foret; quas uirtutes quanto plus in nobis habemus, tanto propius sumus Deo, et maiorem nostri conditoris / gerimus similitudinem. 30v

13. IN. Si autem, quod absit, nostrum aliquis per deuia uitiorum, et diuortia criminum ab hac nobilissima sui conditoris similitudine degener oberrat, quid ei futurum esse adseris?

RESP. Absit, ut hoc fiat! Nam si forsitan euenerit, quid aliud, nisi ut impleatur in nobis, quod scriptum est: *Homo, cum in honore esset, non intellexit, conparatus est iumentis insipientibus, et similis factus est illis*? Quae maior honor potuit homini esse, quam ut ad similitudinem sui factoris conderetur et eisdem uirtutum uestimentis ornaretur, quibus et conditur de quo legitur: *Dominus regnauit, decore indutus est*, id est, omnium uirtutum splendore et totius bonitatis decore ornatus. Et econtra: quod maius ei potest esse dedecus, aut infelicior miseria, quam ut hac similitudinis gloria sui condi-

143–145 *Homo... illis*: Ps 48:13
148 *Dominus... est*: Ps 92:1

140 diuortia: deuortia *MS*

toris amissa ad informem et inrationabilium brutorum iumentorum delabatur similitudinem. Quapropter, o dilectissime frater, adtende diligentius primae conditionis nostrae excellentiam, et uenerandam sanctae Trinitatis agnosce imaginem, honoremque similitudinis diuinae, ad quam creatus es, nobilitatem morum, exercitium uirtutum, dignitatem morum meritorumque / habere 31r contende, ut quando appareat qualis sit, tunc similis ei appareas, qui te mirabiliter ad similitudinem suam in primo Adam condidit, mirabiliusque in secundo reformauit. Haec de imagine et similitudine habeto.

14. IN. Expleta ratione imaginis ad similitudinem interioris hominis, quae cunctis, sicut hucusque retulisti, praecedit creaturis, qualis eius natura sit secundum rationem exterioris hominis, uelut quid ipsa natura dicatur, diligenter expone.

RESP. Natura dicta est ab eo, quod nasci aliquod faciat, gignendi enim et faciendi potens est. Hanc quidam Deum esse dixerunt, a quo omnia creata sunt et existunt.

15. IN. Quid est 'genus'?

RESP. 'Genus' est a 'gignendo' dictum, cui diriuatiuum nomen a terra, ex qua omnia gignuntur.

16. IN. Quomodo?

RESP. *Ge* enim Grece 'terra' dicitur.

17. IN. 'Vita' unde dicitur?

RESP. 'Vita' dicta est propter 'uigorem,' uel quod uim teneat nascendi atque crescendi, unde et arbores uitam habere dicuntur, quia gignuntur et crescunt.

18. IN. 'Homo' unde est dictus?

RESP. Ideo enim 'homo' est appellatus, quia ex humo est factus; sicut et in Genesi dicitur: *Et creauit Deus hominem* / 31v *de humo terrae*. Abusiue autem pronuntiatur ex utraque substantia

161 End of the section drawn from the *Dicta Albini*. Questions 14–88 (lines 162–482) are based on Isidore, *Etymologiae* 11.1.1–35, ed. in W.M. Lindsay, *Isidori Hispalensis Episcopi Etymologarium Sive Originum Libri XX*, 2 vols. (Oxford, 1911).

173 *Ge*: Latinization of the Greek *γῆ*.

180–181 *Et…terrae*: Gen 2:7

153 delabatur: delabitur *MS* **167** quidam: quaedam *MS* **171** qua: quo *MS* **178** Homo: omo *MS* **181** pronuntiatur: ponitur *MS*

totus homo, id est, ex societate animae et corporis; nam proprie homo ab humo.

19. IN. 'Homo' quomodo uocatur Grece?

RESP. Greci autem hominem *antrophum* appellauerunt, eo quod sursum exspectet subleuatus ab humo ad contemplationem artificis sui, quod Obidius poeta designat, cum dicit:

> Pronaque conspectant animalia cetera terram,
> Hos homines sublime dedit caelumque uidere
> Iussit et erectos ad sidera tollere uultus.

20. IN. Cur homo aspicere caelum dicitur?

RESP. Ideo enim erectus ad caelum aspicit, ut Deum quaerat, non ut terram intendat, ueluti pecora, quae natura prona et uentribus oboedientia finxit.

21. IN. Est homo simplex an duplex?

RESP. Homo autem duplex est, interior et exterior.

22. IN. Quomodo?

RESP. Interior homo anima; et exterior homo, corpus.

23. IN. 'Anima' unde nomen accepit?

RESP. A gentilibus enim anima nomen sumpsit, eo quod uentus sit, unde et 'uentus' Grece *anemos* dicitur, quod ore trahentes aerem uiuere uideamur, sed apertissime falsum est.

24. IN. Qua ratione?

RESP. Quia multo prius / gignitur anima, quam concipi aer 32r
<ore> possit, quia iam in genetricis utero uiuit, et ideo non

185 *antrophum*: Latinization of the Greek ἄνθρωπον.

187 Obidius: the poet Ovid (43 BC–AD 17/18)

188–190 Ovid, *Metamorphoses*, 1.84–86 (with variations). This passage, a favorite of medieval authors, was frequently quoted in similar contexts throughout the early middle ages, as in Bede, *In Genesim* 1.1.26. The source for the quotation is not the *Metamorphoses* itself (though manuscripts of the text circulated in Carolingian Francia as early as the ninth century) but Isidore's *Etymologies* 11.1.5. On knowledge of the *Metamorphoses* during this period, see L.D. Reynolds, ed. *Texts and Transmission: A Survey of the Latin Classics* (Oxford, 1984), 276–282.

201 *anemos*: Latinization of the Greek ἄνεμος.

193–194 uentribus: uentris *MS* **202** uiuere: uidere *MS* **205** ore *supplied from MSS BCD*

est aer anima, quod putauerunt quidam, quia non potuerunt incorpoream eius cogitare naturam.

25. IN. Dic mihi, si idem sit spiritus quod et anima?

RESP. Spiritum idem esse quod et animam euangelista pronuntiat dicens: *Potestatem habeo ponendi animam meam, et rursus potestatem habeo sumendi eam.* De hac quoque ipsa Domini anima passionis tempore memoratus euangelista ita protulit dicens: *Et inclinato capite emisit spiritum.* Et idcirco nihil aliud est spiritum emittere, nisi quod et animam ponere.

26. IN. Quare dicta est 'anima'?

RESP. Anima est enim dicta propter quod uiuit.

27. IN. Quare uocatur 'spiritus'?

RESP. Spiritus autem appellatus est uel pro spiritali natura uel pro eo, quod inspiret in corpore.

28. IN. Inter animum et animam quid interest?

RESP. Animus idem est quod et anima; sed anima uitae est, animus consilii. Vnde dicunt philosophi etiam sine animo uitam manere et sine mente durare animam, unde et amentes; nam mentem uocari, ut sciat, animum uero, ut uelit. / 32v

29. IN. Mens unde uocatur?

RESP. Mens autem uocata, quod emineat in animam uel quod meminit. Vnde et inmemores amentes. Quapropter non anima sed quod excellit in anima mens uocatur, tamquam caput eius uel oculus, unde et homo ipse secundum mentem imago Dei dicitur. Ita autem haec omnia adiuncta sunt animae, ut una res sit; pro efficientiis enim causarum diuersa nomina sortita est anima. Nam et memoria mens est, unde et inmemores amentes.

30. IN. Qua ratione?

RESP. Cum ergo uiuificat corpus, anima est; dum uult, animus est; dum scit, mens est; dum recolit, memoria est; dum rectum iudicat, ratio est; dum spirat, spiritus est; dum aliquid sentit, sensus est: nam inde animus sensus dicitur pro his, quae sentit, unde et sententia nomen accepit.

210–211 *Potestatem…eam*: Io 10:18
213 *Et…spiritum*: Io 19:30
224 *animum…uelit*: note that this clause is still controlled by the 'dicunt' at the beginning of the sentence.

206 quia: quae *MS* **221** uitae: uita *MS* **224** animum: anima *MS*

31. IN. ‘Corpus’ unde dictum est?

RESP. Dictum est enim ‘corpus,’ eo quod ‘corruptum perit’; solubile enim atque mortale est, et aliquando soluendum.

32. IN. Vnde dicta est ‘caro’?

RESP. ‘Caro’ autem a ‘creando’ est appellata.

33. IN. Quomodo?

RESP. Crementum enim semen est masculi, / unde animalium 33r
et hominum corpora concipiuntur; hinc et parentes creatores uocantur.

34. IN. Quibus ex causis constat caro?

RESP. Caro autem ex quattuor elementis conpacta est.

35. IN. Quibus?

RESP. Nam terra in carne est; aer in alitu, humor in sanguine, ignis in calore uitali; habent enim in nobis elementa suam quaeque partem, cuius quid debetur conpage resoluta.

36. IN. Inter carnem et corpus quid interest?

RESP. Caro enim et corpus diuersa significant.

37. IN. Quomodo?

RESP. In carne semper corpus est, non semper in corpore caro.

38. IN. Qua ratione?

RESP. Nam caro est quae uiuit idem et corpus; corpus quod non uiuit idem non caro.

39. IN. Quomodo?

RESP. Nam corpus dicitur aut quod post uitam est mortuum aut sine uita est conditum. Interdum et cum uita corpus et non caro, ut herba et lignum.

40. IN. Sensus corporis quot sunt?

RESP. Quinque.

41. IN. Quomodo uocantur?

RESP. Visus, auditus, odoratus, gustus, et tactus.

42. IN. Qui ex his aperiuntur et clauduntur, qui uero sunt patentes?

RESP. Oculi et os aperiuntur et clauduntur; aures uero et / nares 33v
patentes existunt.

251 *alitu*: viz. ‘halitu.’

253 *cuius…resoluta*: ‘some of which must be rendered [i.e. restored to the earth] when the structure dissolves.’

257 non: nam *MS*

43. IN. Quare 'sensus' uocantur?

RESP. 'Sensus' sunt dicti, quia per eos anima subtilissime totum corpus agitat uigore sentiendi, unde et 'praesentia' nuncupantur, quod sint 'prae sensibus'; sicut 'prae oculis,' quae praesto sunt oculis.

44. IN. Quid est uisus?

RESP. Visus est, qui a philosophis humor uitreus appellatur.

45. IN. Visus unde sit?

RESP. Visum autem fieri quidam adseuerant aut extrema aetheria luce aut interno spiritu lucido per tenues uias a cerebro uenientes atque penetratis tunicis in aere exeuntes, et tunc conmixtione similis materiae uisum dantes.

46. IN. Vnde dicitur 'uisus'?

RESP. 'Visus' est dictus, eo quod uiuatior sit ceteris sensibus ac praestantior siue uelocior, ampliusque uigeat, quantum memoria inter cetera mentis officia; uicinior est enim cerebro, unde omnia manant. Ex quo fit, ut ea, quae ad alios pertinent sensus, uidere dicamus, ueluti cum dicimus: 'Vide quomodo sonat,' 'uide quomodo sapit,' sic et cetera.

47. IN. 'Auditus' quare appellatur?

RESP. 'Auditus' est appellatus eo quod uoces hauriat, hoc est, aere uerberato suscipiat / sonos. 34r

48. IN. Quare dicitur 'odoratus'?

RESP. Dicitur enim 'odoratus,' quasi aeris odoris adtactus. Tacto enim aere sentitur, sic et olfactus, quod odoribus afficiatur.

49. IN. 'Gustus' unde appellatur?

275–277 *unde...oculis*: 'thus things are called "present" because they are "before the senses"; likewise, things present to the eyes are "before the eyes."'

281–284 *Visum...dantes*: 'Indeed, some claim that vision is created by external light in the air or by a radiant inner spirit that travels through slender passages from the brain and, after it has passed through the outer membranes, enters the air and generates vision after mixing with a similar substance.' The text here refers to the so called 'emission theory of vision,' according to which visual perception derives from the eyes emitting light rather than receiving it ('intromission theory').

287 praestantior: praestatior *MS*

RESP. 'Gustus' enim a 'gutture' est dictus.

50. IN. 'Tactus' quare uocatur?

RESP. 'Tactus' dictus est, eo quod pertractet et tangat, et per omnia membra uigorem sensus aspergat. Nam tactu probamus quicquid ceteris sensibus iudicare non possumus.

51. IN. Genera tactus quot esse dicuntur?

RESP. Duo.

52. IN. Quae?

RESP. Aut enim extrinsecus uenit, quod feriat, aut intus in ipso corpore oritur, ut sentiatur.

53. IN. Habet unusquisque sensus propriam naturam an non?

RESP. Habet quidem.

54. IN. Qua ratione?

RESP. Quod enim uiuendum est, oculis capitur; quod audiendum, auribus; quam mollia et dura, tactu aestimantur; sapor uero gustu; odor autem naribus ducitur.

55. IN. Quae est prima pars hominis?

RESP. Prima pars corporis caput.

56. IN. Quare ita uocatur?

RESP. Ideo enim datum est illi hoc nomen, eo quod et sensus omnes et nerui inde initium capiant, atque ex eo omnis uigendi
causa oriatur; / ibi enim omnes sensus apparent, unde ipsius 34v
animae, quae consulit corpori, quodammodo gerit personam.

57. IN. Quid est uertix?

RESP. Vertix est ea pars, qua capilli capitis colliguntur, et in qua cessaries uertitur, unde et nuncupatur.

58. IN. Quid est caluaria?

RESP. 'Caluaria' est dicta ab ossibus caluis per defectionem, et neutraliter pronuntiatur.

59. IN. Quid est opcipitium?

327–328 *Caluaria...pronuntiatur*: '"skull" is so called from its bones that are bald [*calvus*] through a deficiency [of hair], and is treated as a neuter [noun].'

329 *opcipitium* = occipitium. See the same word in the subsequent line also. The assimilation of opc– into occ– follows the same pattern as obc– into occ–.

302 pertractet: pertractat *MS* **324** qua capilli: quae capillis *MS*

RESP. Opcipitium est capitis pars posterior, quasi contra capitium, uel quod sit capitis retrorsum.

60. IN. Vnde dicuntur 'capilli'?

RESP. 'Capilli' sunt uocati quasi 'capitis pili,' facti ut et decorem praestent et cerebrum aduersus frigus muniant atque a sole defendant.

61. IN. 'Pili' quare uocantur?

RESP. Dicti sunt autem 'pili' a 'pelle,' de qua prodeunt; sicut et 'pilum' dicitur a 'pila,' ubi pigmentum contunditur.

62. IN. 'Cesaries' unde appellantur?

RESP. 'Cesaries' a 'cedendo' est uocata, ideoque tantum uirorum est.

63. IN. Quare uirorum et non feminarum?

RESP. Quoniam uirum decet tonsum esse, mulierem non decet.

64. IN. Quid sunt comae?

RESP. 'Comae' sunt propriae noti cessi capilli, et est sermo Grecus.

65. IN. Qua ratione?

RESP. 'Comas' enim Greci *caimos* a secando nominant; unde
et *cyrin* tondere / dicunt. Inde et cirri uocantur; quod etiam 35r
idem Greci *mallonem* uocant.

66. IN. 'Crines' unde uocantur?

RESP. Crines autem proprie mulierum sunt, et dictae 'crines' eo quod uittis discernuntur, unde et 'discriminalia' dicuntur, a quibus diuisae religantur.

67. IN. Quid sunt tympora?

RESP. Tympora sunt quae caluariae dextra laeuaque subiacent.

68. IN. Quare ita uocantur?

RESP. Ideo sic nuncupantur, quia mouentur, ipsaque mobilitate quasi tempora a quibusdam interuallis mutantur.

345–346 *Comae… Grecus*: 'Properly, "hair" [*comae*] is hair [*capilli*] that has not been cut, and is a Greek word.'

348 *caimos*: Latinization of the Greek κόμην.

349 *cyrin*: Latinization of the Greek χείρειν.

350 *mallonem*: Latinization of the Greek μαλλόν.

355 *tympora*: viz. tempora

349 tondere: tundere *MS* **356** laeuaque: leuaque *MS*

69. IN. Quare dicta est 'facies'?
RESP. 'Facies' ab 'effigie' est dicta, ubi est enim tota figura hominis, et uniuscuiusque personae cognitio.

70. IN. Quare dicitur 'uultus'?
RESP. 'Vultus' dictus est, eo quod per eum uoluntas animi ostenditur.

71. IN. Qua ratione?
RESP. Secundum uoluntatem enim in uarios motus mutatur, unde et differunt sibi utraque. Nam 'facies' simpliciter accipitur de uniuscuiusque naturali aspectu; 'uultus' autem animorum qualitatem significat.

72. IN. 'Frons' unde nomen accepit?
RESP. 'Frons' enim ab oculorum foraminibus nominata est; haec imago quaedam animi mentisque motum specie sua exprimit, dum uel / laeta uel tristis est. Haec tibi, frater mi, de 35v ratione humanae naturae hac uice sufficient.

73. IN. Ista mihi sufficiunt, sed si placet, reuertamur ad rationem spiritus, de quo paulo superius iam aliquid protulisti, et inuestigemus, in quantum Deo permittente ualeamus, quod spiritus idem creator omnium creasset?
RESP. Difficilis res est ad inuestigandum, sed tamen faciamus, ut dicis.

74. IN. Dic ergo mihi, quot spiritus uitales esse credantur?
RESP. Secundum quod legi, tres spiritus uitales creauit omnipotens Deus.

75. IN. Qui sunt hi?
RESP. Vnus est, qui carne non tegitur; alius, qui carne tegitur sed non cum carne moritur; tertius uero, qui carne tegitur et cum carne moritur.

76. IN. Nunc rogo, ut mihi aperias, qui ex his non tegitur carne; et carne tegitur sed non cum carne moritur; qui uero carne tegitur et cum carne moritur; seu etiam unusquisque eorum ad quam pertineat creaturam?

382–396 The responses to questions 74–76 are condensed from Gregory I, *Dialogues* 4.3, ed. Adalbert de Vogüé, *Gregory the Great: Dialogorum libri quatuor de miraculis patrum Italicorum*, 3 vols., Sources Chrétiennes (Paris, 1978–1980).

361 Facies: Aacies *MS*

RESP. Spiritus namque, qui carne non tegitur, angelorum est; spiritus autem, qui carne tegitur sed non cum carne moritur, hominum est; spiritus uero, qui carne tegitur et cum carne moritur, iumentorum omniumque / brutorum animalium est. 36r

77. IN. Habentur plures spiritus, an non?

RESP. Vtique habentur.

78. IN. Quomodo?

RESP. Dicitur etiam et pars animae, id est rationabilis mens quae oculus est animae, spiritus, quae capax est donorum spirituum et diuinae inhabitationis gratiam obtinet participando, sicut Apostolus ait: *Renouamini spiritu mentis uestrae.* Et iterum: *Si uiuimus spiritu, spiritu et ambulemus.* Et item: *Vos autem in carne non estis, sed in spiritu.*

79. IN. Est ibi aliquid amplius ad requirendum?

RESP. Etiam.

80. IN. Quid?

RESP. Dicitur quoque generaliter tota anima spiritus, sicut de Domino in Euangelio scriptum est: *Inclinato capite tradidit spiritum.* Et Psalmus de hominibus: *Exiuit spiritus eorum.* Et Ecclesiastes: *Quis nouit, si spiritus filiorum Adam ascendit*

393–396 A parallel to this response can be found in the the pseudo-Isidorian *Questiones tam de nouo quam de uetere testamentum*: 'Dic mihi. Quantos uel qualis spiritus creauit omnipotens Deus? Respondit. Tribus. Vnum, qui carnem [sic] non tegitur, id est angelorum. Alium, qui carnem [sic] tegitur et non cum carnem [sic] morietur, id est hominum. Tertium, qui carnem [sic] tegitur et cum carnem [sic] morietur, id est iumentorum et brutorum animalium. Homo itaque sicut in medio creatus est, ut essit [sic] inferior angelorum, superior iumentorum.' Ed. Robert McNally, *Scriptores Hiberniae Minores, Pars I.* Corpus Christianorum Series Latina, vol. 108B (Turnhout, 1973), 201–202.

397 The remaining question and answer sets in this chapter have a greater density of Scriptural citations than elsewhere in the *Disputatio*, raising the possibility that this section is an originally separate composition incorporated into the present text.

403 *Renouamini… uestrae*: Eph 4:23

404 *Si… ambulemus*: Gal 5:25

404–405 *Vos… spiritu*: Rom 8:9

410–411 *Inclinato… spiritum*: Io 19:30

411 *Exiuit… eorum*: Ps 18:5

412–413 *Quis… sursum*: Eccl 3:21

sursum. Dicuntur, sicut superius dixi, animae omnium animalium spiritus, de quibus idem Ecclesiastes ait: *Quis nouit, si spiritus iumentorum descendat deorsum*. Et in fine Psalmorum, unde iam dictum est: *Omnis spiritus laudet Dominum*. In Hebraico enim legitur: *Omne quod spirat, laudet Dominum*. Et in Genesi: *Omnis caro, quae habeat spiritum / uitae*. Dicitur 36v
enim uocalis flatus in homine spiritus, sicut Apostolus ait: *Nam si orem lingua, spiritus quidem meus orat, mens autem mea sine fructu est*.

81. IN. Adhuc de ratione spirituum a te audire uoluissem. RESP. Et ego tibi, prout scio, adhuc dicam. Dicitur quoque flatus uentorum spiritus, sicut scriptum est: *Spiritus procellarum*. Et alibi: *Spiritu uehementi conteres naues Tharsis. Adduxit quoque Dominus spiritum super terram, et inminutae sunt aquae*. Dicuntur et aduersariae potestates spiritus, sicut scriptum est: *Spiritus Domini malus inruebat in Saul*. Et iterum: *Cum inmundus spiritus exierit ab homine*. Dicitur etiam motus animi uel ad excitationem uel ad submissionem spiritus.

82. IN. Quomodo ad excitationem?

RESP. Ad excitationem namque, sicut diximus, hominem tumentem spiritu; aut sicut dicitur, spiritus superbiae, spiritus uanae gloriae.

83. IN. Quomodo ad submissionem?

414–415	*Quis... deorsum*: Eccl 3:21
416	*Omnis... Dominum*: Ps 150:6 as it appears in Jerome's translation of the Septuagint.
417	*Omne... Dominum*: Ps 150:6 as it appears in Jerome's translation of the Hebrew.
418	*Omnis... uitae*: Gen 7:15
419–421	*Nam... est*: 1 Cor 14:14
424–425	*Spiritus procellarum*: Ps 10:7; Ps 148:8
425	*Spiritu... Tharsis*: Ps 47:8
426–427	*Adduxit... aquae*: Gen 8:1
428	*Spiritus... Saul*: 'The evil spirit of the Lord came upon Saul.' A paraphrase of 1 Reg 18:10 taken from Isidore's *Sententiae* 3.5.6.
429	*Cum... homine*: Mt 12:43

425 Spiritu: Spiritus *MS* **426–427** inminutae: diminutae *MS*

RESP. Ad submissionem quoque, sicut in bonam partem: *In spiritu humilitatis*, et, *beati pauperes spiritu*. Et Apostolus de sermone Dei dicit, quod sit *pertingens usque ad diui-*
sionem animae, ac spiritus. Iuxta / quem talem modum di- 37r
citur et diuina animaduersio spiritus, sicut scriptum est: *En proferam uobis spiritum meum, et ostendam uerba mea*. Et iterum, iniqui dicuntur, *flante Deo perisse, et spiritu irae eius esse consumptos*, quod utique non proprie dicitur de Deo, sed metaforice ab humanis motibus translatum est ad Deum.

84. IN. Inueniuntur alii esse spiritus, an non?

RESP. Scriptum est etiam de sole: *Gyrans gyrando uadit spiritus*. Vel sicut alia habet translatio: *Lustrans uniuersa per circuitum pergit spiritus*. Sed de his superioribus modis patet ueritas, quae dicantur spiritus; de hoc quoque, quod sol spiritus dicitur, non declarat, quare dicatur, teste beato Augustino, qui ait: 'Dicant qui possunt,' et reliqua.

85. IN. His ita expletis, supplico caritatem tuam, ut mihi ueraciter aperias, si in sanctis Scripturis plures spiritus sim ausus inuestigare?

RESP. Vtique.

86. IN. <Q>ua ratione?

RESP. Summus namque conditor et uiuificator Spiritus omnipotens Deus propter spiritalem et incorpoream naturam

437–438 *In... humilitatis*: Mt 5:3
438 *beati... spiritu*: Mt 5:3
439–440 *pertingens... spiritus*: Hebr 4:12
441–442 *En... mea*: Prov 1:23
443–444 *flante... consumptos*: Job 4:9
448–450 The author of the *Disputatio* here offers two different renderings of Eccle 1.6. The latter ('Lustrans uniuersa...') is taken from the Vulgate, while the former ('Gyrans gyrando...') occurs in Jerome, *Commentarius in Ecclesiasten* 1.6; *Commentarius in Ezechielem* 1.1; *Commentarius in Zachariam* 2.prol.; Isidore, *De natura rerum* 3.4; and Bede, *De temporum ratione, liber* 8. The *Disputatio* author's immediate source is unclear.
452–453 Augustine, *Enchiridion* 15.58.

439 sit: si *MS* **440** talem: tale *MS*

spiritus dicitur, sicut Veritas in Euangelio ait: *Spiritus est Deus, et eos, qui adorant eum, in spiritu et ueritate oportet / ado-* 37v
rare. Dicuntur enim dona gratiarum spiritus, sicut euangelista testatur cum uerbis Domini, qui ait: *Flumina de uentre eius fluent aquae uiuae*; subiungit: *Hoc autem dicebat de spiritu, quem accepturi erant credentes in eum*. Hoc modo Spiritus Sanctus mentium habitator esse dicitur, sicut Apostolus ait: *Corpora uestra templum est Spiritus Sancti*. Et post pauca: *Glorificate et portate Deum in corpore uestro*. Et alibi: *Caritas Dei diffusa est in cordibus nostris per Spiritum Sanctum, qui datus est nobis*. Haec de spiritibus habeto.

87. IN. Prolata ratione spirituum nunc uolo ut dicas mihi, quibus nominibus in Scripturis sacris <Deus uocetur qui est spiritus omnium spirituum.

RESP. In scripturis et enim sacris> decim nomina Deus habere legitur.

88. IN. Quae sunt haec?

RESP. Primum apud Hebreos nomen Dei 'El' dicitur, secundum 'Eloi,' tertium 'Eloe,' quartum 'Sabaoth,' quintum 'Elion,' sextum 'Eiei,' septimum 'Adonai,' octauum 'Ia,' nonum tetragrammaton, quod est 'Iode Iode,' decimum uero 'Sadai.'

89. IN. Nunc rogo ut horum omnium rationem atque interpretationem, de quibus dixisti, quare uocentur, mihi exponas.

RESP. Secundum quod legi, faciam quod petisti. Primum apud Hebreos Dei / nomen, sicut dixi, 'El' dicitur, quod alii 38r

461–463 *Spiritus…adorare*: Io 4:24
464–465 *Flumina…uiuae*: Io 7:38
465-466 *Hoc…eum*: Io 7:39
467–468 *Corpora…Sancti*: 1 Cor 6:19
468–469 *Glorificate…uestro*: 1 Cor 6:20
469–471 *Caritas…nobis*: Rom 5:5
483 The remainder of this chapter derives from *Etymologiae* 7.1, which Isidore describes as particularly indebted to Jerome's *De decem nominibus dei* (7.1.1: 'Beatissimus Hieronymus, vir eruditissimus et multarum linguarum peritus, Hebraeorum nominum interpretationem primus in Latinam linguam convertit').

473–475 Deus uocetur…enim sacris: *C*

'Deum,' alii aethimologiam eius exprimentes 'Chyros,' id est 'fortem,' interpretati sunt, ideo quod nulla infirmitate obprimitur, sed fortis est et sufficiens ad omnia perpetranda. Secundum nomen, 'Eloi,' tertium 'Eloe,' quod utrumque in Latinum 'Deus' dicitur; est autem nomen in Latinum ex Greca appellatione translatum. Nam 'Deus' Grece 'Theos' dicitur, id est 'timor,' unde tractum est nomen 'Deus,' quod eum colentibus sit timor. 'Deus' autem propriae nomen est Trinitatis, pertinens ad Patrem et Filium et Spiritum Sanctum. Ad quam Trinitatem etiam reliqua, quae infra Deum sunt posita, uocabula referuntur. Quartum nomen Dei dicitur 'Sabaoth,' quod uertitur in Latinum 'exercituum' siue 'uirtutum,' de quo in psalmo ab angelis dicitur: *Quis est iste rex gloriae, Dominus uirtutum.* Sunt enim in huiusmodi ordinatione uirtutes multae, ut angeli, archangeli, principatus, et potestates, cunctique caelestis militiae ordines, quorum tamen et ille Dominus est. Omnes enim sub ipso sunt, eiusque dominatui subiacent. Quintum 'Elion,' quod interpretatur in Latinum / 'excelsus,' qui 'supra caelos' est, sicut scriptum est de 38v
eo: *Excelsus Dominus, super caelos gloria eius.* 'Excelsus' autem dictus 'pro ualde celsus,' 'ex' enim pro 'ualde' ponitur, quasi 'eximius,' quasi ualde eminens. Sextum 'Eiei,' id est 'qui est'; Deus enim solus qui aeternus 'est,' et ob hoc qui exordium non habet essentia nomen uere tinet. Hoc enim nomen ad sanctum Moysen per angelum est delatum; quaerenti enim, quod esset nomen eius, qui eum pergere praecipiebat ad populum ex Aegypto liberandum, respondit: *Ego sum qui sum, et dices filiis Israhel, qui est, misit me ad uos.* Tamquam in eius conparatione, qui uere est, quia incommutabilis est, ea quae commutabilia facta sunt, quasi non sint; quod enim dicitur 'fuit,' non est, et quod dicitur 'erit,' nondum est. Deus autem 'esse' tantum nouit, 'fuisse' et 'futurum esse' non nouit. Solus enim Pater cum Filio et Spiritu Sancto ueraciter est, cuius

492 *Theos*: Latinization of the Greek θεός.
499–500 *Quis… uirtutum*: Ps 23:8
506 *Excelsus… eius*: Ps 112:4
510 *tinet*: viz. tenet
513–514 *Ego… uos*: Ex 3:14

essentiae comparatum esse nostrum non esse est. Vnde et in conloquio dicimus ‘uiuit Deus,’ quia essentia uita uiuit, quam mors non habet. Septimum ‘Adonai,’ quod generaliter interpretatur ‘Dominus,’ quod dominetur creaturae cunctae, uel quod creatura omnis dominatui eius deseruiat; ‘Dominus’ ergo, et ‘Deus,’ uel quod dominetur omnibus, / uel quod timeatur a 39r
cunctis. Octauum, ‘Ia,’ quod in Deo tantum ponitur, quod etiam in ‘Alleluia’ in nouissima syllaba sonat. Nonum tetragrammaton, hoc est quattuor litterarum, quod proprie apud Hebreos in Deo ponitur, ‘Iode Iode,’ id est duabus ‘Ia,’ quae duplicata ineffabile illud et gloriosum Dei nomen efficient. Dicitur autem ineffabilis, non quia dici non potest, sed quia finiri sensu et intellectu humano nullatenus potest, et ideo, quia de eo nihil digne dici potest, ineffabilis est. Decimum uero ‘Sadai,’ id est ‘omnipotens.’ Vocatus autem omnipotens, eo quod omnia potest, sed a faciendo quod uult, non a patiendo, quod non uult. Quod si acciderit, nequaquam esset omnipotens; facit enim quicquid uult et inde omnipotens. Item ‘omnipotens,’ quia ipsius sunt omnia, quae ubique sunt; solus enim totius mundi habet imperium.

90. IN. Est licitum plura nomina Dei inquirere, an non?

RESP. Licet utique.

91. IN. Quomodo?

RESP. Dicuntur etiam et alia quaedam in Deum substantialiter nomina, ut inmortalis, incorruptibilis, incommutabilis, aeter-
nus, / unde et merito cunctae praeponitur creaturae. Dicitur 39v
etiam inuisibilis, inpassibilis, simplex, incorporeus, inmensus et perfectus.

92. IN. Quare dicitur inmortalis?

RESP. Dicitur etiam ‘inmortalis,’ sicut de eo scriptum est: *Qui solus habet inmortalitatem*, quia in eius natura nulla est commutatio; nam omnis mutabilitas non inconuenienter mortalitas dicitur, secundum quod et anima dicitur mori, non quia in corpus uel in aliquam alteram substantiam mutatur et uertitur,

520 The two occurences of ‘esse’ in this sentence should both be taken as nouns.

521–522 *quia…habet*: ‘because his being lives with a life over which death has no hold.’

549–550 *Qui…inmortalitatem*: 1 Tim 6:16

sed in ipsa sua substantia quicquid alio modo nunc est aut fuit, secundum id quod destitit esse quod erat, mortalis itaque deprehenditur; ac per hoc solus Deus dicitur inmortalis, quia solus est incommutabilis.

93. IN. Quare dicitur incorruptibilis?

RESP. 'Incorruptibilis' appellatur, quia corrumpi et dissolui non potest nec diuidi; quicquid enim capit diuisionem, et interitum capit. Ille nec diuidi potest, nec interimi, unde incorruptibilis est.

94. IN. Vnde dicitur incommutabilis?

RESP. Incommutabilis inde est, quia semper manet et mutari nescit; nec proficit, quia perfectus est, / nec deficit, quia aeter- 40r
nus est.

95. IN. Quomodo est aeternus?

RESP. Quia sine tempore est; non enim habet initium neque finem. Hinc et sempiternus, eo quod sit semper coaeternus.

96. IN. Vnde dicitur aeternus?

RESP. A quibusdam autem aeternus ab 'ethere' creditur dictus, quoniam caelum sedes eius habetur, unde est illud: *Caelum caeli Domino*, et reliqua.

97. IN. Quare dicitur inuisibilis?

RESP. Quia numquam per substantiam suam apparuit oculis mortalium Trinitas, nisi per speciem subiectae creaturae eiusdemque corporeae; nam nemo potest ipsam manifestationem essentiae Dei uidere et uiuere, sicut et dictum est Moysi. Vnde et Dominus in Euangelio dicit: *Deum nemo uidit umquam.* Res est enim inuisibilis, ideoque non oculo sed corde quaerendus est.

98. IN. Quomodo est inpassibilis?

554–557 *sed in ipsa sua ... incommutabilis*: 'But anything is deemed to be mortal which, in its own substance, is now or was previously something different because it ceases to be what it was; thus for this reason God alone is said to be immortal because he alone is immutable.'

572–573 *Caelum... Domino*: Ps 113:16

578 *sicut... Moysi*: Ex 33:20

579 *Deum... umquam*: Io 1:18

576–577 eiusdemque: eandemque *MS*

RESP. Quia nullis perturbationibus afficitur, quibus fragilitas humana subcumbit; non enim adtingunt eum ullae passiont libido, iracundia, cupiditas, timor, meror, inuidia, et cetera, quibus mens humana / turbatur. Sed cum dicitur Deus irasci 40v
aut zelari aut dolere, nostro usu dicitur. Apud Deum enim perturbatio nulla est, apud quem tranquillitas summa est.

99. IN. Quare uocatur simplex?

RESP. 'Simplex' dicitur siue non amittendo quod habet, seu quia non aliud est ipse et aliud quod in ipso est, sicut in homine, cuius aliud est esse et aliud sapere. Nam et esse potest, et sapiens non esse; Deus autem habet essentiam, habet et sapientiam, sed quae habet, hoc et est, et omnia unus est, ac proinde simplex est, quia non in eo aliquid accidentis est, sed et quod est et quod in ipso est essentialiter est, excepto quod relatiue ad quamcumque personam est. Summe bonus, quia incommutabilis est; creatura uero bonum sed non summum est, quia mutabilis est; et dum sit quidem bonum, non tamen esse potest et summum.

100. IN. Quare dicitur incorporeus?

RESP. Ideo 'incorporeus,' uel 'incorporalis' Deus dicitur, ut spiritus credatur uel intellegatur esse, non corpus. Nam dum dicitur 'spiritus,' eius significatur substantia.

101. IN. Quare 'inmensus' appellatur?

RESP. Quia ille cuncta concludit / et a nemine concluditur, sed 41r
omnia intra eius potentiam coartantur.

102. IN. Quare dicitur perfectus?

RESP. Quia nihil possit ei adici. Adtamen de consummatione alicuius facti perfectio dicitur.

103. IN. Deus autem, qui non est factus, quomodo potest esse perfectus?

RESP. Hoc uocabulum ex usu nostro sumpsit humana inopia, sicut et reliqua.

104. IN. Quare idem uocatur 'creator'?

RESP. Dictus est enim 'creator' pro totius mundi rebus ab ipso creatis; nihil enim est, quod non originem a Deo traxerit. Ipse et unus, quia diuidi non potest, uel quia nihil aliud esse potest, quod tantundem capiat potestatis. Haec igitur, quae de

597 bonus: bonum *MS* **603** esse: est *MS*

Deo hucusque dicta sunt, ad totam pertinet Trinitatem propter unam et coaeternam substantiam, siue in Patre, siue in Filio eius unigenito in forma Dei, siue in Spiritu Sancto, quia unus Spiritus est Dei Patris et Filii eius unigeniti.

105. IN. Nunc uoluissem scire, si amplius de nominibus Dei ausus essem inuestigare?

RESP. <Ausus> es, utique.

106. IN. Qua ratione?

RESP. Sunt etiam quaedam uocabula ex usu nostro ad Deum sumpta de membris nostris, siue de inferioribus. Et quia in propria natura in/uisibilis et incorporeus est, pro efficientiis 41v tamen causarum in ipso rerum species adscribuntur, ut more locutionis nostrae facilius seipsum insinuet.

107. IN. Vt hoc intellegere possim, obsecro ut mihi indicare non rennuas?

RESP. Quia omnia uidet recte, dicitur oculus; propter quod omnia audit recte, dicitur auris; pro eo quod auertitur, ambulat; pro eo quod exspectat, stat; sic et in ceteris horum similibus ab humanis motibus trahitur similitudo ad Deum, sicut est obliuiscens et memorans. Hinc est, quod et Propheta dicit: *Iurauit Dominus exercituum per animam suam.*

108. IN. Quomodo per animam iurasse dicitur, cum Deus animam non habet?

RESP. Hoc nostro narrat effectu, sicut et facies Dei in Scripturis sanctis non caro sed diuina cognitio intellegitur eadem ratione, quia per faciem conspectam quisque cognoscitur. Hoc enim in oratione Deo dicitur: *Ostende nobis faciem tuam*; ac si dicatur: 'Da nobis cognitionem tuam.' Sic et 'uestigia Dei' dicuntur, quia nunc Deus per speculum agnoscitur; ad perfectum uero omnipotens repperitur, / dum in futuro facie ad faciem 42r quibusque electis praesentabitur, ut ipsam speciem contemplentur, cuius nunc uestigia conpraehendere conantur, hoc est quem uidere per speculum dicitur. Nam et situs et habitus et locus et tempus non in Deo proprie sed per similitudinem translata

640 *Iurauit...suam*: Ier 51:14
646 *Ostende...tuam*: Ps 79:4

628 nostro ad Deum: nostro ad ad Deum *MS* **636** pro eo: oculus pro eo *MS*

dicuntur; quippe *sedere super Cherubin* dicitur, quod est ad situm; et: *Abyssum tamquam uestimentum amictus*, quod est ad habitum; et: *Anni tui non deficient*, quod ad tempus pertinet; et: *Si ascendero in caelum, tu illic es*, quod ad locum manet; et in Propheta, *plaustri portantis faenum*, species ad Deum dicitur. Et haec omnia per figuram Deus, quia nihil est horum ad proprietatem substantiae eius. Haec tibi de Dei nominibus hucusque sufficiant.

III. DE SEX AETATIBVS MVNDI, MAIORIS VIDELICET ET MINORIS

1. IN. Haec mihi sufficiunt, sed quoniam a senario numero haec disputatio nostra coepit initium, inquiramus ex parte rationem sex aetatum mundi, et quae earum ratio sit, et quot generationes uel quot anni / in unaqueque earum contineatur, 42v
ut breuiter mihi exponas obsecro.

RESP. De generationibus earum, prout donante Domino possim, soluam; de annis uero, sicut nosti, diuersi diuersa sentiunt, attamen iuxta quod ex ipsis inuenire ualui, tuae fraternitati respondebo. Prima aetas fuit, nisi fallor, ab Adam usque ad Noe, continens generationes X, annos secundum Hebraeos MDCLVI, secundum LXX interpretes MMCCXLII. Secunda a Noe usque ad Abraham, continens similiter generationes X, Christi secundum carnem generationes XIIII, anni uero iuxta

654	*sedere... Cherubin*: Ps 98:1
655	*Abyssum... amictus*: Ps 103:6
656	*Anni... deficient*: Ps 101:28
657	*Si... es*: Ps 138:8
658	*plaustri... faenum*: Am 2:13
669–680	The text of this response is culled from Isidore, *Etymologiae* 5.38–39, though much reduced. Differences between the lengths given for each age in the *Etymologiae* and those found here suggest that the *Disputatio* author also consulted Bede's *De temporibus* XVI (ed. in Christopher W. Jones, *Bedae Venerabilis Opera: Pars I, Opera Didascalia*. Corpus Christianorum Series Latina, vol. 123B (Turnhout, 1977), 585–611, at 600–601.
674	*LXX interpretes*: the seventy translators of the Septuagint Bible.

660 *MS D ends here.* **674** MDCLVI: IDCLCVI *MS* | MMCCXLII: IICCXLII *MS*

Hebreos DLXXXVIIII. Sexta siquidem, quae nunc agitur, nulla generationum uel temporum serie certa, sed ut aetas decrepita ipsa totius saeculi morte finienda. Ecce habes in paucis, quae de aetatibus mundi maioris quaesisti.

2. IN. Ista recipio, / si tamen dicere uoluisses, quot sint 43r
aetates mundi minoris?

RESP. Totidem sunt, ut reor, quot et maioris.

3. IN. Et si totidem sunt, quomodo nominantur uel quae est earum ratio, aut quot annis continentur?

RESP. Prima earum infantia est pueri nascentis ad lucem, septem continens annos; nam infans dicitur homo primae aetatis, eo quod adhuc fari, id est loqui nescit. Secunda pueritia est pura et necdum ad generandum apta, tendens usque ad XIIII annum. Tertia adolescentia ad gignendum adulta, quae porrigitur usque ad XXVII annos. Quarta iuuentus, firmissima aetatum omnium, finiens in quinquagesimo anno. Quinta aetas senior, id est grauitas, quae est declinatio a iuuentute in senectutem, nondum tamen senectus, sed iam nondum iuuentus; haec enim aetas a quinquagesimo anno incipiens, in septuagesimo terminatur. Sexta aetas senectus, quae nullo annorum tempore finitur, sed post quinque illas aetates quantumcumque uitae est, senectuti deputabitur.

4. IN. Quid nobis sentiendum est de hoc, quod legitur in
psalmo: *Et usque in senectam / et senium*? 43v

RESP. 'Senium' enim pars est ultima senectutis dicta, quod sit terminus sextae aetatis. Haec de aetatibus habeto.

IIII. DE RATIONE TEMPORVM

Domine, quoniam omnes aetates et omnia saecula, sicut optime nostis, per diuersa spatia temporum transeunt atque discurrunt, si placet, uolumus auxiliante Domino de eisdem temporibus,

686–698 The account of the six ages of man derives from *Etymologiae* 11.2.1–8.

700 *Et…senium*: Ps 120:18

702 End of the material based on *Etymologiae* 11.2.8

704–708 The MS does not specify a speaker here. It may be that this passage was meant to serve as a prayer in the style of a collect.

679–680 quae de aetatibus: quae de ea aetatibus *MS*

prout intellegimus, in praesentia uestra aliquid habere disputationis.

1. IN. Dic, frater karissime, horum temporum ratio sub quot capitulis continetur, in quantum nunc ad nostram pertinet disputationem?
RESP. Nisi fallor sub X capitulis consistere cernitur.

2. IN. Quae sunt haec?
RESP. Primum capitulum est de Chronicae uocabulo, secundum de momentis et horis, tertium de diebus, quartum de nocte, quintum de ebdomadis, sextum de mensibus, septimum de solstitiis et aequinoctiis, octauum de temporibus anni, nonum de annis, decimum de olympiadibus et lustris et iubeleis.

3. IN. Ecce protulisti numerum et nomina capitulorum. Nunc peto ut mihi aperire non rennuas, qua lingua 'Chronica' appellatur?
RESP. Certe, frater, quia humiliter / petisti ea quae scire cu- 44r
pis, ego autem quod intellego amabiliter tibi indicare cupio. 'Chronica' Grece dicitur, quae Latine 'temporum series' appellatur.

4. IN. Quis eam conposuit?
RESP. Eusebius enim Caesariensis episcopus apud Grecos illam edidit, sed Hieronimus Pater in Latinam linguam illam

714–718 This account matches the ten chapters that Isidore has on the subject. The topics listed in the response quote the headings in the *Etymologiae* almost exactly. With few exceptions, the rest of this chapter of the *Disputatio* is culled from *Etymologiae* 5.28–37.

727 St. Eusebius (ca. AD 260–340), bishop of Caesarea and author of the *Chronicon*, a chronicle of world history from the lifetime of Abraham through the twentieth year of the reign of the Roman Emperor Constantine I (AD 325).

728 St. Jerome (ca. AD 347–420) authored a continuation of Eusebius' world chronicle extending its coverage from AD 325 to 379. On the medieval reception of Eusebius' and Jerome's chronicles, see Andrew Rabin, 'Historical Re-Collections: Rewriting the World Chronicle in Bede's *De Temporum Ratione*,' *Viator* 36 (2005) 24–34.

719 nomina: *corr. from* noma *MS*

conuertit. 'Chronos' enim Grece, Latine 'tempus' interpretatur.

5. IN. Tempora in quot partes diuiduntur?

RESP. In sex.

6. IN. In quibus?

RESP. In momentis, horis, diebus, mensibus, annis, et lustribus.

7. IN. Quid est momentum?

RESP. Momentum est minimum atque angustissimum tempus a motu siderum dictum. Est enim extremitas horae in breuibus interuallis, cum aliquid sibi cedit atque succedit.

8. IN. 'Hora' qua lingua dicitur?

RESP. 'Hora' Grecum nomen est, et tamen Latinum sonat.

9. IN. Quid est hora?

RESP. Finis ėst temporis, sicut et hora sunt finis maris, fluuiorum, et uestimentorum.

10. IN. Quid est dies?

RESP. Dies est praesentia solis siue sol supra terras, sicut nox sol sub terris.

11. IN. Quomodo?

RESP. Vt enim dies aut nox sit, causa est, ut supra terram sol aut sub terris.

12. IN. Dies / quot horas habet? 44v

RESP. Dies legitimus XXIIII horarum est, usque dum dies et nox spatio sui cursus ab oriente usque ad alium orientalem solem caeli uolubilitate concludit; nam abusiue dies unus est spatium ab oriente sole usque ad occidentem.

13. IN. Diei spatia quot sunt?

RESP. Duo.

14. IN. Quae?

RESP. Interdianum atque nocturnum. Et est dies quidem horarum XXIIII, spatium autem horarum XII.

15. IN. Vnde dicitur 'dies'?

RESP. Vocatus est autem 'dies' a parte meliore, unde et in usu est, ut sine commemoratione noctis numerum dicamus dierum,

729 *Chronos*: Latinization of the Greek Χρόνος.

743 *hora*: viz. ora

sicut et in lege diuina scriptum est: *Factum est uespere et mane dies unus.*

16. IN. Dic mihi, quibus horis secundum consuetudinem uniuscuiusque gentis rationem inchoat dies?
RESP. Secundum Aegyptios incipit ab occasu solis, secundum Persas ab ortu solis, secundum Athenienses a VI hora diei, secundum Romanos uero a media nocte, unde et tunc 'gallicinium' est, quorum uox diei ostendit praeconium, quando et mesonictios afflatus fit.

17. IN. Vnde dicti sunt 'dies'?
RESP. 'Dies' a 'diis' sunt dicti, quorum nomina Romani quibusdam sideribus sacrauerunt.

18. IN. Qua ratione? / 45r
RESP. Primum enim diem a sole appellauerunt, qui princeps est omnium siderum, sicut et idem dies caput est cunctorum dierum. Secundum a luna, quae soli et splendore et magnitudine proxima est, et ex eo mutuat lumen. Tertium ab stella Martis, quae uesper uocatur. Quartum a stella Mercurii, quam quidam candidum circulum dicunt. Quintum ab stella Iouis, quam Foetonem aiunt. Sextum a Veneris stella, quam Luciferum adserunt, quae inter omnia sidera plus lucis habet. Septimum uero ab stella Saturni, quae sexto caelo locata XX annis fertur explere cursum suum.

19. IN. Quare ab his VII stellis dies nominati sunt?
RESP. Ideo enim ex his VII stellis nomina dierum gentiles dederunt, quia per easdem aliquid sibi effici existimarunt, dicentes habere a sole spiritum, a luna corpus, a Mercurio ingenium et linguam, a Venere uoluptatem, a Marte sanguinem, a Ioue temperantiam, a Saturno humorem. Talis quippe extitit gentilium stultitia, qui sibi finxerunt / tam ridiculosa figmenta. 45v

20. IN. Quomodo uocatur dies apud Hebreos?
RESP. Apud Hebreos autem dies prima 'una sabbati' dicitur, qui apud nos dies Dominicus est.

21. IN. Secunda sabbati quare appellatur?

764–765 *Factum… unus*: Gen 1.5
771–772 *quando…fit.*: 'when the midnight breeze begins.'

780 mutuat: mutat *MS*

RESP. Secunda sabbati secunda feria, quem saeculares diem lunae uocant.

22. IN. Quid est tertia?

RESP. Tertia sabbati tertia feria, quem diem illi Martis uocant.

23. IN. Quid est quarta?

RESP. Quarta sabbati quarta feria est, qui Mercurii dies est a paganis.

24. IN. Quid est quinta?

RESP. Quinta sabbati quinta feria est, id est quinta a die Dominico, qui apud gentiles Iouis uocatur.

25. IN. Quid est sexta?

RESP. Sexta sabbati sexta feria dicitur, qui apud eosdem paganos Veneris uocatur.

26. IN. Sabbatum quid est?

RESP. Sabbatum aut septimus a Dominico die est, quem gentiles Saturno dicauerunt, et Saturnum nominauerunt.

27. IN. 'Sabbatum' quid interpretatur?

RESP. 'Sabbatum' autem ex Hebreo in Latinum 'requies' interpretatur, eo quod in eo Deus requieuisset ab omnibus operibus suis. Melius autem in uocabulis dierum de ore Christiano ritus loquendi ecclesiasticus procedit. Tamen si quem forte consuetudo traxerit, ut illud exeat ex ore, quod inprobat corde, / 46r
intellegat illos omnes, de quorum nominibus appellati sunt hi dies, homines fuisse; et propter beneficia quaedam mortalia, quia plurimum potuerunt et eminuerunt in hoc saeculo, delati sunt eis ab amatoribus suis diuini honores et in diebus et sideribus. Sed primum a nominibus hominum sidera nuncupata, et a sideribus dies sunt appellati.

28. IN. Vnde dicuntur 'feriae'?

RESP. 'Feriae' autem a 'fando' sunt nuncupatae, quod sit in eis nobis tempus dictionis, id est in diuino uel humano officio fari. Sed ex iis festi dies institute sunt hominum causa: feriati, causa divinorum sacrorum.

819 The corrected text here and below follows the parallel passage in Isidore: *Etymologiae* 5.30.11.

819 quod: qui *MS* **821** et propter beneficia: et pro beneficiis *MS* **824** a nominibus: ab hominibus *MS* **829–830** Sed…sacrorum: Sed ex his festis diebus hominum causa institutos feriatos diuinorum sacrorum. *MS*

29. IN. Partes diei quot sunt?
RESP. Tres.

30. IN. Quae sunt hae?
RESP. Mane, meridies, et supprema.

31. IN. Quomodo mane?
RESP. Mane lux matura et plena, nec iam crepusculum.

32. IN. Quare dicitur 'mane'?
RESP. 'Mane' autem a 'manu' est dictum.

33. IN. Qua ratione?
RESP. 'Manum' enim antiqui bonum dicebant; quid enim melius luce? Alii mane existimant uocari ab animabus, quorum conuersatio a luna ad terram est. Alii putant ab aere, quia 'manus,' id est clarus atque perspicuus.

34. IN. 'Meridies' quare / uocatur? 46v
RESP. 'Meridies' dicta quasi 'medidies,' hoc est 'mediusdies,' uel quia tunc purior dies est. 'Merum' enim 'purum' dicitur; in toto enim die nihil clarius meridie, quando sol in medio caelo rutilat, et omnem orbem pari claritate inlustrat.

35. IN. Quid est 'subprema'?
RESP. 'Subprema' est postrema pars diei, quando sol cursum suum in occasum uertit; et dicta 'subprema,' quod superest ad partem ultimam diei.

36. IN. 'Serum' quare dicitur?
RESP. 'Serum' uocatum est a 'clausis seris,' quando iam nox uenit, et unusquisque somno tutior fit.

37. IN. Cur dicitur 'hodie'?
RESP. 'Hodie,' quasi 'hoc die,' sic et 'quottidie,' non 'cotidie,' ut sit quot diebus. Alicubi aliter legitur, 'non a quota die, sed a continenti die "cotidie" dicitur.'

841–842 *ab animabus…est*: Isidore's text reads, 'a manibus quorum conversatio a luna ad terram est.' It appears the scribe has misread 'manibus' and attempted to rationalize the error.

858–859 The last sentence of this response ('Alicubi…dicitur') is found only in Alcuin's *De orthographia* (*PL* 101:915). Although much of Alcuin's text is in turn derived from Bede's orthographical treatise of the same name, this particular sentence is found only in Alcuin. On this passage, see the Introduction, pp. 9–10.

842 ab aere: habere *MS*

38. IN. 'Cras' quare appellatur?

RESP. 'Cras,' quod est 'postea.' Externum est pridie, et dictum 'externum' ab eo, quod iam dies ipse sit a nobis extraneus et praetereundo alienus.

39. IN. Vnde dicitur 'pridie'?

RESP. 'Pridie' autem dictum quasi 'priori die.' <Perindie,> id est per ante diem, uel in 'antecessum,' id est 'prius.'

40. IN. Vnde dicta est 'nox'?

RESP. 'Nox' a 'nocendo' est dicta, eo quod oculis noceat.
Quae idcirco / lunae ac siderum lucem habet. Ne indecora es- 47r
set, consolarentur omnes nocte operantes, et ut quibusdam animantibus, quae lucem solis ferre non possunt, ad sufficientiam temperaretur.

41. IN. Alternatio diei ac noctis cur facta est?

RESP. Noctis autem et diei alternatio propter uicissitudinem dormiendi uigilandique effecta est, et ut operis diurni laborem noctis requies temperet.

42. IN. Quare facta est nox?

RESP. Aut quia longa itinera lassatur sol, et cum ad ultimum caeli spatium peruenit, elanguescit, ac tabefactus efflat suos ignes: aut quia eadem ui sub terras cogitur, qua super terras pertulit lumen, et sic umbra terrae noctem facit. Vnde et Virgilius:

Ruit Oceano nox,
Inuoluens umbra magna terramque polumque.

43. IN. Partes noctis quot sunt?

RESP. Septem.

44. IN. Quae?

RESP. Vesper, crepusculum, conticinium, intempestum, gallicinium, matutinum, et diluculum.

45. IN. Quid est 'uesper'?

861 *Externum*: viz. Hesternum

883–884 Virgil, *Aeneid* 2.250–251. Virgil's works did circulate in eighth- and ninth-century Francia, though as was the case with Ovid, the passages cited in the *Disputatio* are taken from Isidore's *Etymologiae* rather than direct reference to the *Aeneid*. See Reynolds, *Texts and Transmission: A Survey of the Latin Classics*, 433–437.

880 eadem: eodem *MS*

RESP. ‘Vesperum’ ab stella occidentali uocatum, quae solem
occiduum sequitur, et tenebras sequentes / praecedit, de qua 47v
Virgilius:

> Ante diem clauso conponit Vesper Olimpo.

46. IN. Vnde sunt ‘tenebrae’ dictae?

RESP. Quod teneant umbras.

47. IN. Quid est ‘crepusculum’?

RESP. Crepusculum est dubia lux. Nam creperum dubium dicimus, hoc est inter lucem et tenebras.

48. IN. Quid est ‘conticinium’?

RESP. Conticinium est, quando omnes silent; conticescere enim silere est.

49. IN. Quid est ‘intempestum’?

RESP. Intempestum est medium et inactuosum, quod est tempus quando agi nihil potest, et omnia sopore quieta sunt. Nam tempus per se non intellegitur, nisi per actus humanos. Nam medium noctis actu caret: ergo ‘intempesta’ inactuosa, quasi sine tempore, hoc est sine actu, per quem dinoscitur tempus. Vnde est: ‘Intempestiue uenisti.’ Ergo ‘intempesta’ dicitur, quia caret tempora, id est actuum.

50. IN. Quid est ‘gallicinium’?

RESP. ‘Gallicinium’ propter gallos, lucis praenuntios dictum.

51. IN. Quid est ‘matutinum’?

RESP. Matutinum est inter abscessum tenebrarum et aurore aduentum, et dictum ‘matutinum,’ quod hoc tempus inchoante mane sit.

52. IN. Quid est / ‘diluculum’? 48r

RESP. ‘Diluculum’ quasi incipiens parua diei lux. Haec et aurora, quae solem praecedit. Est autem aurora diei clarescentis

894 Virgil, *Aeneid* 1.378.

909 *Intempestiue uenisti*: this phrase, which also appears in Isidore, is a colloquial expression without a known source.

914 *aurore* should be read as a genitive (‘aurorae’).

904 quod: *corr. from* quad *MS* **907** intempesta: tempestas *MS* **909** intempesta: tempesta *MS* **912** praenuntios: praenuntiatio *MS* *(The corrected text follows the parallel passage in Isidore.)*

exordium et primus splendor aeris, qui Grece *Eos* dicitur. Nam nos per diriuationem 'auroram' uocamus, quasi 'Eoruram.' Vnde est illud:

> Splendidus auctoris de uertice fulget Eous.

53. IN. Quare dicitur 'ebdomada'?

RESP. 'Ebdomada' dicta a numero septem dierum, quorum repetitione et menses et anni et saeculum peraguntur.

54. IN. Qua ratione?

RESP. *Epta* enim Greci 'septem' dicunt. Hanc nos 'septimanam' uocamus, quasi 'septem lucis.' Nam 'mane' lux est.

55. IN. Vnde appellatur 'octauus dies'?

RESP. Octauus autem dies, id est primus, ad quem reditur et a quo rursus ebdomadis series oritur.

56. IN. 'Mensis' unde uocatus?

RESP. 'Mensis' nomen est Grecum de lune nomine tractum.

57. IN. Quomodo?

RESP. 'Luna' enim *mene* Greco sermone uocatur. Vnde et apud Hebreos menses legitimi non ex solis circulo sed ex lune cursu enumerantur, quod est de noua / ad nouam. Aegyptii autem 48v
primi propter lune uelociorem cursum, et ne error computationis eius uelocitate accideret, [non] ex solis cursu diem mensis adinuenerunt, quoniam tardior solis motus facilius poterat conpraehendi.

58. IN. 'Ianuarius' quare uocatur?

920 *Eos*: Latinization of the Greek ἠώς.

923 *Eous*: Sedulius Scottus, *Carmen Paschale* 5.191. Instead of Sedulius, Isidore illustrates 'Eos' with Virgil, *Aeneid* 1.489 ('Et laetus Eoos Eurus equis') and II. 417 ('Eoasque acies'). In contrast to MS A, B and C combine the quotations from Isidore and Sedulius, substituting 'laetus' for 'splendidus auctoris' to produce the phrase 'laetus de vertice fulget Eous.' The wording of the response—'alicubi aliter legitu'—suggests that the author was perhaps familiar with, and had read, Sedulius' work. The different treatments of this passage support the argument that B and C derive from a different manuscript recension than A.

928 *Epta*: Latinization of the Greek ἑπτά.

936 *mene*: Latinization of the Greek μήνη.

940 uelocitate: uelocitati *MS*

RESP. Ianuarius mensis a 'Iano' est dictus, qui fuit a gentilibus ei consecratus, uel quia limes et ianua sit anni. Vnde et bifrons idem Ianus pingitur, ut introitus anni et exitus demonstretur.

59. IN. 'Februarius' unde appellatur?

RESP. Februarius nuncupatur a 'Februa,' id est Plutone, cui eo mense sacrificabatur. Nam Ianuarium diis superis; Februarium diis Manibus Romani consecrauerunt. Ergo Februarius a Februa, id est Plutone, non a 'febre,' quod est aegritudo, nominatur.

60. IN. 'Martius' unde appellatur?

RESP. 'Martius' appellatus est propter Martem Romanae gentis auctorem: uel quod eo tempore cuncta animantia agantur ad marem et ad concumbendi uoluptatem.

61. IN. Quomodo aliter uocatur?

RESP. Appellatur autem idem et mensis nouorum, quia anni
initium mensis est / Martius; idem et nouum uer ab indiciis sci- 49r
licet germinum, quia in eo uiridantibus fructibus nouis trans-
actorum probatur occasus.

62. IN. 'Aprelis' unde dicitur?

RESP. Aprelis est pro uenere dicitur, quasi 'afrondis.'

63. IN. Quomodo?

RESP. Grece enim 'Afrodis' Venus dicitur, uel quia in hoc mense omnia aperiuntur in florem, quasi 'aperilis.'

64. IN. 'Maius' unde uocatur?

RESP. 'Maius' dictus a Maia, matre Mercurii, uel a maioribus natu, qui erant principes reipublicae. Nam hunc mensem maioribus, sequentem uero minoribus Romani consecrauerunt, unde et 'Iunius' dicitur. Antea enim populus in centurias seniorum et iuniorum diuisus erat.

65. IN. 'Iulius' et 'Augustus' unde sunt dicti?

RESP. Iulius uero et Augustus de honoribus hominum Iulii et Augusti Caesaris nuncupati sunt.

66. IN. Quomodo uocabantur prius?

RESP. Prius enim 'Quintilis' et 'Sextilis' uocabantur.

963 *afrondis*: Isidore's text reads 'Aphrodis,' that is 'Aphrodite.' A Latinization of the Greek 'Αφροδίτη.

946 idem: id est *MS* **956** concumbendi: concubendi *MS* **959** idem: id est *MS* | nouum uer: nouember *MS* **965** Afrodis: Afrondis *MS* **975** Caesaris: Caesares *MS*

67. IN. Qua ratione?

RESP. 'Quintilis,' quia quintus erat a Martio, quem principem anni testantur esse Romani; 'Sextilis' uero similiter, quod sit sextus.

68. IN. 'September' unde nomen accepit?

RESP. September enim nomen habet a numero et 'imbre,' / 49v
quia septimus est a Martio et imbres habet; sic et October, Nouember, atque December ex numero et imbribus acceperunt uocabula. Quem numerum decurrentem December finit, pro eo quod denarius numerus praecedentes numeros claudit.

69. IN. 'Kalendae,' 'Nonae,' et 'Idus' quare uocantur?

RESP. Kalendas autem, Nonas, et Idus propter festos dies Romani instituerunt, uel propter officia magistratuum.

70. IN. Qua ratione?

RESP. In his enim diebus conueniebant in urbibus.

71. IN. Cur specialiter nominatae sunt?

RESP. Quidam autem Kalendas a 'colendo' appellari existimant. Apud ueteres enim omnium mensuum principia colebantur, sic et apud Hebreos. Idus autem plerique Latinorum ab 'edendo' dictum putant, quod hi dies apud ueteres aepularum essent. Nonae a 'nondinis' uocatae. Nondinae autem sunt publicae conuentiones siue mercimonia.

72. IN. 'Solesticium' quare dicitur?

RESP. 'Solesticium' dictum quasi solis statio, quod tunc / sole 50r
stante crescant dies uel noctes.

73. IN. Quare dicitur 'aequinoctium'?

RESP. 'Aequinoctium' appellatum est, quod tunc dies et nox horarum spatio aequali consistunt.

74. IN. Solestitia quot sunt?

RESP. Duo.

75. IN. Quae?

RESP. Vnum aestiuum octauo Kalendarum Iuliarum, de quo tempore remeare sol ad inferiores incipit circulos. Aliud hiemale octauo Kal. Ian., quo tempore sol altiores incipit circulos petere. Vnde et hiemalis solestitii dies minimus, sicut aestiui maximus inuenitur.

995 *mensuum*: alternate spelling of 'mensium.'

1009 *octauo…Iuliarum*: viz. June 24th.

1011 *octauo Kal. Ian.*: viz. December 25th.

76. IN. Aequinoctia quot sunt?

RESP. Duo.

77. IN. Quae?

RESP. Vnum uernale et aliud autumnale, quae Greci *Isimrias* uocant.

78. IN. Haec aequinoctia quo tempore fiunt?

RESP. Vnum est die octauo Kal. Aprilium, alter uero octauo Kal. Octobrium, quia annus olim in duas tantum partes diuidebatur, hoc est in aestiuum et in hiemale solstitium, in duo emispheria.

79. IN. Anni tempora quot sunt?

RESP. Quattuor.

80. IN. Quae?

RESP. Primum est uer, secundum aestas, tertium autumnus, et quartum hiems.

81. IN. Vnde / dicuntur 'tempora'? 50v

RESP. Dicta sunt autem tempora a 'communionis temperamento,' quod inuicem se humore, siccitate, calore, et frigore temperent.

82. IN. Quomodo aliter uocantur?

RESP. Dicuntur enim 'curricula,' quia non stant sed currunt.

83. IN. Qua ratione?

RESP. Constat autem post factum mundum ex qualitate cursus solis tempora in ternos menses fuisse diuisa, quorum temporum talem ueteres discretionem faciunt, ut primum mensem uer 'nouum' dicitur, secundum 'adultum,' tertium uero 'praeceps.' Sic et aestas in suis tribus mensibus noua, adulta, et praeceps. Item hiems noua, adulta, et praeceps, siue extrema, unde et est illud: 'Extreme sub casu hiemps.'

84. IN. 'Ver' unde appellatur?

1017 *Isimrias*: Latinization of the Greek ἰσημερίας.

1020 *octauo Kal. Aprilium*: viz. March 25th. It should be noted that both Isidore and the author of the *Disputatio* dated the equinoxes according to the Julian calendar. Under the Gregorian calendar instituted in 1582, the vernal equinox can vary from the 19th to the 21st of March and the autumnal equinox can vary from the 21st to the 24th of September.

1020–1021 *octauo... Kal. Octobrium*: viz. September 24th.

1042 *Extreme... hiemps*: the *Disputatio*'s construction here follows that in the *Etymologiae*. Virgil, *Georgics* 1.340 with variations.

RESP. 'Ver' autem dictum, quod 'uiret.' Tunc enim post hiemem uestitur tellus herbis, et in florem cuncta rumpuntur.

85. IN. 'Aestas' unde dicitur?

RESP. 'Aestas' dicitur ab 'estu,' id est a 'calore'; et 'aestas' quasi 'usta,' id est exusta et arida. Nam calor aridus est.

86. IN. 'Autumnus' unde appellatur?

RESP. 'Autumnus' a tempestate uocatus, quando et folia arborum / cadunt, et omnia maturescunt. 51r

87. IN. 'Hiems' quare dicitur?

RESP. 'Hiems' est ratio emisferii nuncupata.

88. IN. Quomodo?

RESP. Quia tunc breuiori uoluitur circulo. Vnde et hoc 'tempus bruma' dicitur, quasi *braxin*, id est 'breuis,' uel a 'cibo,' quod maior sit tunc uescendi appetitus.

89. IN. Qua ratione?

RESP. Edacitas enim Grece *bruma* appellatur. Vnde et 'inbrumati' dicuntur, quibus fastidium est ciborum.

90. IN. 'Hibernus' quare ita uocatur?

RESP. Hibernus autem inter hiemem et uernum, quasi 'hiuernus,' qui plerumque a parte totam hiemem significat.

91. IN. Haec tempora cui deputantur?

RESP. Adscribuntur enim singulis partibus caeli.

92. IN. Quomodo?

RESP. Ver quippe orienti datur, quia tunc ex terris omnia oriuntur. Aestas uero meridiano, eo quod pars eius calore flagrantior sit. Hiems septemtrioni, eo quod frigoribus et perpetuo gelu torpet. Autumnus occiduo, propter quod graues morbos habet, unde et tunc omnia folia arborum defluunt. Vt autem autumnus abundet morbis, facit hoc / confinium frigoris et caloris et 51v
coṇpugnantia intra se contrariorum aerum.

93. IN. Annus quid est?

RESP. Annus est solis anfractus, cum peractis trecentis sexaginta quinque diebus ad eadem loca siderum redit.

94. IN. Vnde dicitur 'annus'?

1053 *ratio* here should be understood as 'principle' or 'condition.'

1056 *braxin*: Latinization of the Greek *βραχύν*.

1059 *bruma*: Latinization of the Greek *βρῶμα*.

1055 uoluitur: soluitur *MS* **1072** morbis: morbos *MS*

RESP. 'Annus' dictus est, quia mensibus in se recurrentibus uoluitur. Vnde et 'anulus,' quasi 'annuus,' id est 'circulus,' quod in se redeat, unde et Virgilius:

> Atque in se sua per uestigia uoluitur annus.

Sic enim apud Aegiptios indicabatur ante inuentas litteras picto dracone caudam suam mordente, quia in se recurrit. Alii annum dicunt *apotilnanystai*, id est 'ab inuocatione, renouatur enim semper.'

95. IN. Quot sunt aliter annorum tempora?

RESP. Annorum tempora tria sunt.

96. IN. Quae sunt haec?

RESP. Aut enim lunaris est annus, qui continet dies XXX, aut solstitialis, qui continet XII menses, aut magnus omnibus planetis in eundem locum recurrentibus, quod fit post annos solestitiales plurimos.

97. IN. Quid est aera, uel quis eum constituit?

RESP. Aera singulorum annorum / est constituta a Cesare Au- 52r
gusto, quando primum censu exagitato Romanum orbem descripsit.

98. IN. Vnde dicitur 'aera'?

RESP. Dicta est autem 'aera' ex eo, quod omnis orbis aes reddere professus est reipublicae.

99. IN. 'Olimpias' unde dicitur?

RESP. Olimpias apud Grecos est constituta apud Elidem Grecie ciuitatem, Eliis agentibus agonem et quinquennalem certamen, quattuor mediis annis uacantibus; et ob hoc Elidum certaminis tempus 'olimpiadem' uocauerunt, quadriennio in una olimpiade subputato.

1081 *Atque…annus*: Virgil, *Georgics* 2.402.

1084 *apotilnanystai*: Latinization of ἀνανεοῦσθαι.

1090–1092 *magnus…plurimos*: the 'Great Year' referred to here (also known as a 'Platonic Year' as it was first described in Plato's *Timaeus*) is the length of time it takes the moon and planets to complete at least one full cycle around the sun and one complete axial revolution and return to the same position in relation to each other, a period of approximately 28,500 solstitial years.

1082 indicabatur: iudicabatur *MS* **1083** mordente: mordentem *MS* **1093** eum: ea *MS*

100. IN. Quid est lustrum?
RESP. Lustrum est *pentetesin*, id est quinquennium, quod quinto anno dicitur condi propter olimpiades a Romanis. Adhuc enim consules, adhuc non aera erat. Est enim quinquennale tempus.

101. IN. Quare ita uocatur?
RESP. Ideo enim sic uocatur, eo quod censu super quinquennium in republicam peracto urbs Roma lustrabatur.

102. IN. Iubeleus quid interpretatur?
RESP. Interpretatur enim 'remissionis annis.' Est enim Hebraicus et sermo et numerus, qui septenis annorum ebdomadibus, id est XL et VIIII annis texitur. In quibus clangebantur / tubae, et ad omnes reuertebatur antiqua possessio, deb- 52v
ita absoluebantur, et confirmabantur libertates. Hunc numerum etiam in diebus Pentecosten et ipsi celebramus post Domini resurrectionem, remissa culpa et totius debiti cirografo euacuato, ab omni nexu liberi suscipientes aduenientem in nos gratiam Spiritus Sancti. Haec pauca tibi de temporum ratione prolata, quousque maiora proferantur, sufficiant.

<V> DE VETERI TESTAMENTO

Quoniam omnia per diuersas temporum successiones ab initio creaturae gesta atque conscripta maxime in Vetere Testamento narrantur atque leguntur, idcirco, si libet, prout nunc occurrit, disputemus inter nos, quae diuersitas atque multiplicitas in eodem Testamento habeatur.

1. IN. Et quia haec ita se aguntur, dic mihi, 'Vetus Testamentum' quare dicatur?
RESP. Vetus enim Testamentum uocatur, quia ueniente Nouo cessauit, sicut ait Apostolus: *Vetera transierunt et ecce omnia*
facta sunt noua. / 53r

2. IN. Vetus enim Testamentum in quot libris dinumeratur?
RESP. In XLV.

3. IN. Quomodo nominantur?
RESP. Genesis, Exodus, Leuiticus, Numeri, Deuteronomius,

1107 *pentetesin*: Latinization of the Greek πεντετηρίν.
1134–1135 *Vetera…noua*: 2 Cor 5:17

1122 liberi: liberis *MS* **1139** Numeri: Numerus *MS*

Iosue, Iudicum, Ruth, Libri Regum IIII, Paralipemenon, Iob, Psalterium, Prouerbiorum, Ecclesiastes, Canticum Canticorum, Libri Prophetarum XVI, Tobi, Iudith, Hester, et Machabeorum.

4. IN. Prolatis numeris quid in unoquoque eorum principaliter contineatur, breui sermone ut mihi aperias, obsecro.
RESP. Prout Domino donante ualeo, faciam.

5. IN. Dic ergo mihi, quid contineatur in Genesi?
RESP. Continetur enim in eo fabrica mundi, conditio hominis, cataclismum, diuisio terrae, confusio linguarum, et gesta omnium Patriarcharum usque ad ingressionem Israhel in Aegyptum.

6. IN. Quid in Exodo?
RESP. Hebreorum seruitus, plaga Aegypti, egressus populi, protectio nubis, transitus Rubri maris, mersus Pharaonis, gloria decantationis, congressus heremi, cibus mannae, fluenta in dulcedinem uersa, pugna Amalech, / mandata decalogi, archam 53v
testamenti, et dedicatio tabernaculi, et oblationis.

7. IN. Quid in Leuitico?
RESP. Lex sacrificiorum et hostiarum diuersitas, indumenta pontificum, ministeria leuitarum, cyborum discretio, diuersitas populorum, purgationesque hostiarum.

8. IN. Quid in Numero?
RESP. Egressio tribuum ex Aegipto et XL duarum per heremum mansionum sacramenta.

9. IN. Quid in Deuteronomio?
RESP. Recapitulatio legis et omnia, quae inter Faran, et Iob, et Laban, et Asaroth usque ad Cadesbarnae fuerunt a Moyse

1146–1299 Questions 5 through 36 of this chapter are, in much abridged form, taken from Isidore's *In libros veteris ac novi testamenti Prooemia* 1–85 (*PL* 83:155–175).

1162 *XL duarum*: the text here refers to the forty-two sites listed in Num 33:3–50 at which the Israelites stopped to rest during their flight from Egypt.

1165–1167 *Recapitulatio…populo*: Deut 1:1–2

1166 *Cadesbarnae*: i.e Kadesh Barnea, a location mentioned in Deut 1:46 as one of the primary encampments of the Israelites during their wanderings in the desert.

1155 archam: archae *MS*

populo: mandata atque promissa, maledictiones peccatorum, et promissiones beatitudinis. Ibi canit canticum Moyses, ibi dat benedictionem filiis Israhel, ibi terra repromissionis conspecta moritur ac sepelitur.

10. IN. Quid in Iesu Naue?

RESP. Transitus Iordanis filiorum Israhel et circumcisio secunda, subuersio Chananeorum, et diuisio terrae eorum, nec non et hereditas sorte suscepta.

11. IN. Quid in libro Iudicum?

RESP. Peccata et seruitus Israhel, exclamationes populi, et miserationes Dei ad eum.

12. IN. Quid in Ruth?

RESP. Istoria / Moabitidis, de cuius stirpe descendit Dauid. 54r

13. IN. Quid in Regum?

RESP. Transitus archae dominicae a Iudaeis ad gentes, sacerdotium Heli, et in Dauid imperium regis Saulis, gesta regum Iudae et Israhelitarum gentium transmigratio quoque ab errore idolatriae Israhel in Assiriis, et aduentus Nabugodonosor in Hierusalem, siue etiam captiuitas principum ac populi, et subuersio urbis uel templi.

14. IN. Quid in Paralipomenon?

RESP. Ordo generationum et temporum, et sanctarum Scripturarum eruditio, nec non et quicquid in historia Veteris Testamenti omissa sunt, aut fortasse non plene degesta, in isto summatim ac breuiter explicata sunt.

15. IN. Quid in Iob?

RESP. Eiusdem sancti uiri damna, funera, uel flagella, et contumeliosa consolantium dicta; lamenta quoque eius, in quibus totius mundi deplorat miseriam; consolatio etiam Dei ad eum per turbinem, et duplex eius in fine remuneratio.

16. IN. Quid in libro Psalmorum?

1171 *Iesu Naue*: an alternate name for the Book of Joshua based on a translation by Origen of the phrase 'son of Nun' into the Greek *υἱὸς Nauê*, which he took to prefigure Jesus' role as the ship of salvation.

1180 *in Regum*: 'libris' is understood.

1167 mandata: data *MS* **1193** funera: funeris *MS*

RESP. Continetur enim in eo allegorice ac tipice sacramenta signata, sed specialiter natiuitas, passio, et resurrectio Christi.

17. IN. Quid in libris Salomonis? / 54v

RESP. In Prouerbiis enim moralia docens per communem quendam loquendi usum altiorem intellegentiam edidit, et conseruationem mandatorum, uel doctrinae caelestis institutionem breuibus sententiis coaptauit. In Ecclesiasten uero rerum naturam discutiens et cuncta in mundo caduca et uana esse repraehendit, rerumque omnium fragilitate perspecta renuntiare mundo ammonuit. In Canticis Canticorum ea, quae sunt caelestia uel diuina sub specie sponsi et sponsae, Christi Ecclesiaeque unitate declarat atque animam ad amorem caelestium excitans et perueniendam ad consortium Dei prouocat.

18. IN. Quid in Prophetis?

RESP. Quamquam multa obscura in eis legantur, quaedam ex eis tibi proferre non denegabo.

19. IN. Dic ergo, quid in Esaia debeo intellegere?

RESP. Occultationem alarum duorum Seraphin sedentium in throno Dei et post uisionem Iudae et Hierusalem aduersus ceteras gentes, quae in circuitu eius sunt, secundum qualitatem locorum et diuersitatem uitae mala, quae eis uentura essent, denuntians, et post captiuitatem Hierusalem ruinam Babyloniae comminatur. / Deinde necem Philistiim, uastationem Moab, 55r
exterminium Damasci, Aegypti commotionem, et solitudinem maris deserti, obsidionem quoque Edom, fugam et interitum Arabiae, excidium uallis Sion, subuersionem etiam Tyri.

20. IN. Quid in Hieremia?

RESP. Locutio simplex, intellectus facilis, imitatio corporis, et in passionibus suis imago exprimitur Redemptoris, destructio regni diaboli, et aedificatio imperii iustitiae uel fidei.

21. IN. Quid in Ezechiel?

RESP. Describuntur enim in eo misteria totius Ecclesiae, quae ex latere Christi formata est.

22. IN. Quid in Danihele?

RESP. Legitur in eo non solum uentura praedicatio, sed etiam definitio temporis incarnationis uel passionis ex ordine regum,

1203 mandatorum: mandatorem *MS* **1215** sedentium: sedentes *MS*

uel numerus annorum, nec non et regnum Antichristi, siue de die iudicii uel regno sanctorum, et in fine eius prophetia Susannae.

23. IN. Quid in Oseae?

RESP. Legitur historialiter ultima credulitas Iudaeorum in Christo et totius Dominicae resurrectionis dies.

24. IN. Quid in Iohel?

RESP. Ille tantum ad Iudam et Hierusalem / uaticinium ferens 55v et <post> uoluptuosa conuiuia ad luctum prouocat Hierusalem, excidiumque eius pronuntiat et uocationem gentium.

25. IN. Quid in Amos?

RESP. Quattuor enim scelera gentium sub totius mundi figuram describens et aduentum Christi omnibus adnuntians.

26. IN. Quid in Abdia?

RESP. Increpatio mystica superbiae Edom, prioris uidelicet populi audaciam, quod Christum occiderit, et futuram salutem Domini.

27. IN. Quid in Iona?

RESP. Figuram gerens passionis mortisque uel resurrectionis Christi, in naufragio uidelicet suo et proiectione de naui in mare. Nec non et de obsorbitione coeti trium dierum ac noctium, uel quod in Nineue paenitentiam mundo praedixerit.

28. IN. Quid in Michea?

RESP. Comminatur Samariae iram Domini ob causam simulacrorum, interitumque uenturum populo Israhelitico denuntiat, et locum, in quo nasceretur Christus, demonstrat.

29. IN. Quid in Naum?

RESP. Pronuntiat simulacra gentium exterminanda, nec non et urbem sanguinum Hierusalem. Post cuius interitum pedes adnuntiantis / pacem, id est Saluatoris aduentum Christi pro- 56r clamat.

30. IN. Quid in Abacuc?

1254 *coeti*: viz. ceti

1263 *urbem sanguinum*: the reference to Jerusalem as a 'city of blood' comes from Nah 3:1.

1234 numerus: numerum *MS* **1235** prophetia: prophetiae *MS* **1254** coeti: coetus *MS*

RESP. In principio uoluminis sui descripsit diabolum cum membris ac moribus suis; in fine uero pronuntiat aduentum et passionem Saluatoris.

31. IN. Quid in Sophonia?

RESP. Praedicat enim contritionem montis Sion, qui est collis Hierusalem, nec non et aliarum gentium euersionem terroremque diei iudicii intonat, et tertium diem resurrectionis Christi prophetat, atque in aduentu Christi totum orbem sub uno iugo Domino seruiturum adnuntiat.

32. IN. Quid in Aggea?

RESP. Restauratio templi Domini, et contritio gentium uel commotio totius mundi, et aduentus Christi seu captiuitas populi.

33. IN. Quid in Zacharia?

RESP. Leguntur enim in eo uisiones diuersae, quae longum est numerare. In quibus etiam diuersa mysteria intellegenda esse noscuntur.

34. IN. Quid in Malachia?

RESP. Demonstrat enim in principio uoluminis sui odium Iudaeorum in Esau et dilectionem minoris populi in Iacob. In
sequentibus autem reprobat Iudeae / uictimas, et sacrificium 56v
transferre adnuntiat; in finem uero aduentum Domini et diem iudicii, iustorumque praemia et impiorum poenas. Iohannis uero aduentum primum et Heliae secundum adnuntiat.

35. IN. Quid in Esdra?

RESP. Renouatio murorum Hierusalem et templi siue altaris, nec non et iuris sacerdotii restitutio seu sanctae religionis culmen multis opibus gentium et principum Persarum muneribus perornatum.

36. IN. Quid in Machabeorum Libris est intellegendum?

RESP. Praenotant enim proelia inter Hebreorum duces et gentes Persarum, pugnamque Sabbatorum et nobiles Machabeorum triumphos, foedus quoque amicitiarum cum Romanorum ducibus actaque legationum.

1284–1285 *Demonstrat…Iacob*: see Mal 1:2–3

1299 This marks the end of the material taken from Isidore's *Prooemia*. The remaining material (questions 37 to 74) is taken from *Etymologiae* 6.1.1, 4–9 and 7.2.1–33.

1274 aduentu: adventum *MS* **1297** pugnamque: pugnaque *MS*

37. IN. Hi libri, de quibus actenus rationem protulisti, in quot ordines secundum Hebreos diuiduntur?
RESP. In tres.

38. IN. Quomodo?
RESP. In lege scilicet, prophetarum et agyographorum.

39. IN. Primus ordo legis quomodo accipiendus est?
RESP. Primus ordo legis in quinque libris accipitur.

40. IN. Qui sunt hi? / 57r
RESP. Primus est 'Bresith,' quod est Genesis; secundus 'Elesmod,' quod est Exodus; tertius 'Vaiecra,' quod est Leuiticus; quartus 'Vagedaber,' quod est Numerus; quintus 'Heliadabarim,' quod est Deuteronomius. Hi sunt quinque libri Moysi, quos Hebrei 'Thorat,' Latini 'Legem' appellant, et haec proprie lex appellatur, quae per Moysen data est.

41. IN. Ordo secundus qualis est?
RESP. Secundus ordo est Prophetarum, in quo continentur libri octo.

42. IN. Quomodo nominantur?
RESP. Primus est 'Iosue Bennon,' qui Latine 'Iesu Naue' dicitur; secundus 'Sopthim,' quod est Iudicum; tertius 'Samuhel,' qui est Regum primus; quartus 'Malachim,' qui est Regum secundus; quintus Esaias; sextus Hieremias; septimus Ezechiel; octauus 'Tharesra,' qui dicitur 'XII prophetarum.' Qui libri, quia sibi pro breuitate adiuncti sunt, pro uno accipiuntur.

43. IN. Qualis est ordo tertius?
RESP. Tertius ordo est agyograforum, id est sancta scribentium dicta, in quo sunt libri nouem.

44. IN. Quomodo uocantur?
RESP. Primus appellatur 'Iob'; secundus 'Psalterium'; tertius

1304 *agyographorum*: 'of the books of the saints'

1308–1311 Listed here are the Hebrew names for the first five books of the Old Testament. The names derive from the first word in each book; hence בְּרֵאשִׁית (*Bereshit*, 'In the beginning') as the title of the text designated *Genesis* in Greek. The other books are שְׁמוֹת (*Shemot*, 'Names,' *Exodus*), ויקרא (*Vayikra*, 'And he called,' *Leviticus*), במדבר (*Bemidbar*, 'In the desert,' *Numbers*), and דְּבָרִים (*Devarim*, 'Words,' *Deuteronomy*).

1305 accipiendus: accipiendum *MS* **1312** proprie: propriae *MS*

'Masloth,' / quod est Prouerbia Salomonis; quartus 'Coeleth,' 58r quod est Ecclesiastes; quintus 'Syrasirim,' quod est Canticum Canticorum; sextus Danihel; septimus 'Dabreiamin,' quod est Verba dierum, hoc est Paralipomenon; octauus Hesdra; nonus Hester. Qui simul omnes quinque, octo, et nouem fiunt XXII, sicut superius dictum est.

45. IN. Habentur plures libri Veteris Testamenti, an non?
RESP. Habentur utique.

46. IN. Qui sunt hi?
RESP. Quidam autem Ruth et Cynoth, quod Latine dicitur 'Lamentatio Hieremiae,' agyografis adiciunt, et XXIIII uolumina Veteris Testamenti faciunt, iuxta XXIIII seniores, qui ante conspectum Domini adsistunt.

47. IN. Inueniuntur amplius ex libris Veteris Testamenti?
RESP. Etiam.

48. IN. Quomodo?
RESP. Habetur etiam ordo quartus eorum librorum, qui in canone Hebraico non sunt.

49. IN. Quomodo uocantur illi?
RESP. Primus est Liber Sapientiae, secundus Ecclesiastes, tertius Tobi, quartus Iudith, quintus, et sextus Machabeorum, quos, licet Iudaei inter apocrifa separent, Ecclesia tamen Christi inter diuinos libros honorat et praedicat.

50. IN. Transactis nominibus et ordinibus, / uel etiam quid 58v ex parte in eisdem libris continetur, nunc obsecro, ut scriptores eorum, qui fuissent, nec non et uocabula, quare unusquisque illorum ita uocetur, mihi aperias.
RESP. Vere, frater, magnam et difficilem rem a me requiris, quam tamen, prout Domino uolente ualeo, tibi exponam.

51. IN. Dic ergo mihi, Veteris Testamenti librorum auctores qui fuissent?
RESP. Veteris Testamenti secundum Hebreorum traditionem hi perhibentur auctores. Primus Moyses diuinae historiae cosmograficon in quinque uoluminibus edidit, quod 'Pentateucum' nominatur.

1348 *Liber Sapientiae*: that is, Ecclesiasticus (Sirach).

1329 *The scribe left fol. 57v blank. The text resumes on fol. 58r.*

52. IN. Quare ita uocatur?

RESP. Pentateucus autem a quinque uoluminibus dicitur.

53. IN. Qua ratione?

RESP. *Penta* enim Grece *theucus* uero uolumen uocatur, ubi et Genesis primus uocatur.

54. IN. Vnde dicitur 'Genesis'?

RESP. Genesis liber inde appellatur, eo quod exordium mundi et generatio saeculi in eo contineatur.

55. IN. 'Exodus' unde nomen accepit?

RESP. Exodus uero exitum ab Aegypto uel egressum populi Israhel digerit, et ex ea causa nomen accepit.

56. IN. 'Leuiticus' unde / dicitur? 59r

RESP. Leuiticus appellatus, eo quod Leuitarum ministeria et diuersitatem uictimarum exsequitur, totusque in eo ordo Leuiticus adnotatur.

57. IN. 'Numeri liber' quare dicitur?

RESP. Numeri liber uocatur, eo quod in eo egressae de Aegipto tribus dinumerantur, et XL ac duarum per heremum mansionum in eo discriptio continetur.

58. IN. 'Deuteronomium' cur ita appellatus est?

RESP. Deuteronomium Greco sermone appellatur, quod Latine interpretatur secunda lex, id est repetitio et euangelicae legis praefiguratio, qui sic ea habet, quae priora sunt, ut tamen noua sint omnia, quae in eo replicantur.

59. IN. 'Iosue' a quo nomen accepit?

RESP. Iosue liber nomen accepit ab Iesu, filio Naue, cuius historiam continet; scriptorem uero eius eumdem Iosue Hebrei adserunt. In cuius textu post Iordanis transitum regna hostium subuertuntur, terra populo diuiditur, et per singulas urbes, uicos, montes, atque confinia Ecclesiae caelestisque Hierusalem spiritalia regna praefigurantur.

60. IN. 'Iudicum' unde nominatur? / 59v

1367 *Penta*: Latinization of the Greek πέντα.
Grece: supply 'quinque' here.
theucus: Latinization of the Greek τεῦχος.

1378 adnotatur: admutatur *MS* **1379** Numeri: Numerus *MS* **1380** Numeri: Numerus *MS*

RESP. Iudicum nominatur a principibus populi, qui praefuerunt in Israhel post Moysen et Iosue, antequam Dauid et ceteri reges existerent. Hunc librum edidisse creditur Samuhel.

61. IN. 'Samuhelis liber,' quare ita appellatur?

RESP. Liber Samuelis eiusdem Samuhelis natiuitatem et sacerdotium et gesta describit, idcirco et ab eo nomen accepit. Et quamuis hic liber Saul et Dauid historiam contineat, utrique tamen ad Samuhelem referuntur, quia ipse unxit Saul in regem, ipse Dauid in regem futurum. Cuius libri primam partem conscripsit idem Samuhel; sequentia uero eius usque calcem scripsit Dauid.

62. IN. 'Malachim' cur ita nominatur?

RESP. Malachim liber proinde appellatur, eo quod reges Iudae et Israheliticae gentis gestaque eorum per ordinem digerat temporum. Malachia Hebraice, Latine 'regum' interpretatur. Hunc librum Hieremias primus in unum uolumen coegit, nam antea sparsus erat per singulorum regum historias.

63. IN. 'Paralipomenon' qua lingua appellatur?

RESP. Paralipomenon Grece dicitur, quae nos / 60r 'praetermissorum uel reliquorum' dicere possumus, quia ea, quae in Lege nec non et in Regum libris uel omissa uel non plena relata sunt, in isto summatim ac breuiter explicantur.

64. IN. Scriptor libri Iob qui fuit?

RESP. Librum Iob quidam Moysen scripsisse arbitrantur, alii unum ex prophetis. Nonnulli uero eundem Iob post plagam suae passionis scriptorem fuisse aestimant, arbitrantes, ut qui certamina spiritalis pugnae sustinuit, ipse narraret quas uictorias expediuit. Principia autem et fines libri Iob apud Hebreos prosa oratione texta sunt; media autem ipsius ab eo loco, qui ait: *Pereat dies, in qua natus sum*, usque ad eum locum: *Idcirco ipse me reprehendo et ago paenitentiam*, omnia heroico metro discurrunt.

65. IN. 'Liber Psalmorum' qua lingua dicitur?

RESP. Psalmorum liber Grece 'Psalterium,' Hebraice 'Nabla,'

1410–1412 *Hunc…historias*: 1 and 2 Reg were originally a single book, but Jerome separated them in the course of compiling the Vulgate.

1425 *Pereat…sum*: Job 3:3

1425–1426 *Idcirco…paenitentiam*: Job 42:6

Latine 'organum' dicitur. Vocatus autem 'Psalmorum liber,' quia uno propheta canente ad psalterium chorus consonando responderet. Titulus autem in Psalmis Hebraicis ita est: 'Hyspysta / librum,' qui interpretatur 'uolumen hymnorum.' Auctores 60v autem psalmorum, qui ponuntur in titulis, Moyses scilicet et Dauid, et Salomon, Asaph, Aethan, et Idithun, et filii Core, Eman Eszrahelitae, et reliquorum, quos Esdras uno uolumine conpraehendit. Omnes autem psalmi apud Hebreos metrico carmine constant esse conpositi. Nam in more Romani Flacci, et Greci Pindari, nunc alii iambico currunt, nunc Eszrahelitae Alchaico personant, nunc Saffico nitent, trimetro uel tetrametro pede incedentes.

66. IN. 'Libri Salomonis' qua ratione consistunt?

RESP. Salomon, filius Dauid, rex Israhel iuxta numerum uocabulorum suorum tria uolumina edidit, quorum primum est 'Masloth,' quem Greci 'Parabolas,' Latini 'Prouerbiorum' nominant, eo quod in ipso sub conparatiua similitudine figuras uerborum et imagines ueritatis ostenderit; ipsam autem ueritatem ad intellegendum legentibus reseruauit. Secundum librum 'Coeleth' uocauit, qui Greci 'Ecclesiasten' dicitur, Latine 'Contionator,' eo quod sermo eius non specialiter ad unum, sicut / in Prouerbiis, sed ad uniuersos generaliter dirigatur docens 61r omnia, quae in mundo cernimus, caduca esse et breuia, et ob hoc minime appetenda. Tertium librum 'Syrasyrin' praenotauit, qui in Latinam linguam uertitur 'Cantica Canticorum,' ubi per epitalamium carmen coniunctionem Christi et Ecclesiae mysticae canit.

67. IN. Quare dicitur 'Cantica Canticorum'?

1432–1433 *Hyspysta*: Isidore has 'Thehilim' instead. The meaning of 'Hyspysta' and the reason for the substitution are unclear.

1436 *Eszrahelitae*: viz. Israelitae

1439 *Flacci*: i.e. Quintus Horatius Flaccus

1439–1440 *nunc…personant*: 'now they resound in the Alcaics of the Israelites'

1453 *Syrasyrin*: an approximate transliteration of שִׁיר הַשִּׁירִים (*Šîr HaššÎrîm*, 'Song of Songs').

1455–1456 *mysticae*: 'mysticae' here should be read as an adverb with a hypercorrected -e.

1431 quia: qui *MS* | chorus: choros *MS*

RESP. Dictum autem 'Canticum Canticorum,' eo quod omnibus canticis praeferatur, qui in Scripturis sacris habentur, sicut quidam in Lege dicuntur sancta, quibus maiora sunt 'sancta sanctorum.' Horum autem trium librorum carmina exametris et pentametris uersibus apud suos conposita perhibentur, ut Iosepus Hieronimusque scribunt.

68. IN. Librum Esaiae quis conposuit?

RESP. Esaias euangelista potius quam propheta, edidit librum suum, cuius omne textum eloquentiae prosa incedit; canticum uero exametro et pentametro uersu discurrit.

69. IN. Hieremiae quis?

RESP. Hieremias similiter edidit librum suum cum Threnis eius, quos nos 'Lamenta' uocamus, eo quod in tristioribus rebus funeribusque adhibeantur. In quibus quadruplicem diuerso / metro 61v
conposuit alfabetum, quorum duo prima quasi Saffico metro scripta sunt, quia tres uersiculos, qui sibi nexi sunt et ab una tantum littera incipiunt, eroicum comma concludit. Tertium alfabetum trimetro scriptum est et a ternis litteris, id est terni uersus, incipiunt. Quartum alfabetum simili primo et secundo habetur.

70. IN. Ezechielis et Danihelis quis?

RESP. Ezechiel et Danihel a uiris quibusdam sapientibus scripti esse perhibentur, quorum Ezechiel principia et fines multis habet obscuritatibus inuoluta. Danihel uero claro sermone regna orbis pronuntiat, et tempus aduentus Christi manifestissima praedicatione adnotat. Hi sunt quattuor prophetae, qui maiores uocantur, quia prolixa uolumina condiderunt.

71. IN. Libri XII Prophetarum auctores qui fuerunt?

RESP. Libri XII Prophetarum auctorum suorum nominibus praenotantur, qui propterea dicuntur minores, quia sermones eorum breues sunt. Vnde et conexi sibimet inuicem in uno uolumine continentur, quorum nomina haec sunt: Osee, Iohel, Amos, Abdias, Ionas, Micheas, Naum, Abacuc, Sophonias, Ageus, Zacharias, et Malachias.

1466 *cuius... incedit*: 'whose entire text proceeds in an eloquent style'

1467 uersu: cursu *MS* **1474** concludit: concludunt *MS (The corrected text follows the parallel passage in Isidore.)* **1479** fines: fine *MS*

72. IN. Esdrae libri / quis auctor extitit? 61*bis* r

RESP. Esdrae liber auctoris sui titulo praenotatur. In cuius textu eiusdem Hesdrae Neemiaeque sermones pariter continentur, ne quemquam moueat, quod unus Esdrae dicitur liber, quia secundus, tertius, et quartus non habentur apud Hebreos, sed inter apocriphos deputantur.

73. IN. Librum Hester quis scripsit?

RESP. Hester librum ipsa creditur conscripsisse, in quo eadem regina sub figura Ecclesiae Dei populum a seruitute et morte eripuisse scribitur atque interfecto hoste Aman, qui interpretatur iniquitas, diei celebritas in posteros mittitur.

74. IN. Libri Sapientiae et Ecclesiastici, Iudith, Tobiae, atque Machabeorum scriptores qui esse dicuntur?

RESP. Liber Sapientiae apud Hebreos nusquam est, unde et ipse titulus Grecam magis eloquentiam redolet. Hunc Iudaei Filonis esse adfirmant, qui proinde 'Sapientia' nominatur, quia in eo est Christi aduentus, qui est 'sapientia Patris,' et passio eius euidenter exprimitur. Librum autem Ecclesiasticum certissime Iesus filius Sirach, Ierosolimita, nepos Iesu sacerdotis magni conposuit, de quo meminit Zacharias. Qui liber apud Latinos propter eloquii similitudinem / Salomonis titulo 61*bis* v
praenotatur. Dictus autem Ecclesiasticus, eo quod totius Ecclesiae disciplinae religiosae conuersationis magna cura et ratione sit edictus. Hic et apud Hebreos repperitur, sed inter apocrifos habetur. Iudith uero et Tobiae siue Machabeorum libri quibus auctoribus scripti sunt, minime constat. Habent autem uocabula ex eorum nominibus, quorum gesta scribunt. Haec pauca de Veteri Testamento hac uice tibi sufficiant.

1491 An error in numbering has caused two successive folia to be labelled fol. 61r–v. See above, p. 7.

1512–1514 *Dictus…edictus*: 'It is called Ecclesiasticus because it has been proclaimed with great care and reason about the teaching of the holy way of life of the entire Church.'

1514 *apocrifos*: Ecclesiasticus (also known as Sirach) is included in the Christian Biblical canon but is not considered part of the Hebrew Bible.

1509 nepos: nepus *MS* **1515** Tobiae: Tobi *MS*

<VI> DE NOVO TESTAMENTO

1. IN. Ea quae de illo dixisti sufficiunt, sed quare Nouum Testamentum dicatur ut mihi aperias, obsecro.
RESP. Nouum Testamentum ideo uocatur, quia innouat; non enim illud discunt, nisi homines renouati ex uetustate per gratiam et pertinentes iam ad testamentum nouum, quod est regnum caelorum.

2. IN. Ordines librorum Noui Testamenti quot sunt?
RESP. Duo.

3. IN. Qui?
RESP. Primus est euangelicus, in quo sunt Matheus, Marcus, Lucas, et Iohannes. Secundus apostolicus, in quo sunt Paulus in XIIII Epistolis, Petrus in duobus, Iohannes in tribus, Iacobus et Iudas in singulis, Actus Apostolorum, et Apocalipsis.

4. IN. Auctores huius Noui Testamenti qui fuerunt? / 62r
RESP. Quattuor libros Euangeliorum quattuor supra nominati singulariter conscripserunt.

5. IN. Nunc peto, ut mihi exponas, quis eorum primus, et qua lingua, uel ubi et unde Euangelium conscripsisset? Similiter de secundo, tertio, et quarto facere non rennuas.
RESP. Primus Mattheus conscripsit Euangelium litteris Hebraicis et sermonibus in Iudaea initiens euangelizare ab humana Christi natiuitate dicens: *Liber generationis Iesu Christi filii Dauid, filii Abraham*, significans descendisse corporaliter ex semine patriarcharum Christum, sicut promissum erat in prophetis per Spiritum Sanctum. Secundus Marcus plenus Spiritu Sancto scripsit Euangelium Christi eloquio Greco in Italia sequutus Petrum ut discipulus. Is initium ab spiritu prophetali fecit dicens: *Vox clamantis in deserto: Parate uiam Domino*, ut ostenderet Christum post adsumptionem carnis Euangelium praedicasse mundo. Ipse enim Christus et propheta dictus est, sicut scriptum est: *Et prophetam in gentibus posui te*. Tertius Lucas inter omnes euangelistas Grecis

1522–1525 Taken from Isidore, *Etymologiae* 6.1.2.
1529–1532 Taken from Isidore, *Etymologiae* 6.1.10.
1533–1586 Questions 4 through 8 of this chapter derive from Isidore, *Etymologiae* 6.2.35–42.
1541–1542 *Liber...Abraham*: Mt 1:1
1547–1548 *Vox...Domino*: Mc 1:3
1550–1551 *Et...te*: Ier 1:5

sermonibus eruditissimus, quippe ut medicus in Grecia, Eu-
angelium scripsit Theophilo episcopo, initians a sacerdotali
spiritu dicens: *Fuit in diebus Herodis regis / Iudaeae sac-* 62v
erdos quidam nomine Zacharias, ut manifestaret Christum
post natiuitatem carnis et praedicationem Euangelii hostiam
fuisse effectum pro salute mundi. Ipse est enim sacerdos, de
quo dictum est in Psalmis: *Tu es sacerdos in aeternum se-
cundum ordinem Melchisedech*. Vbi enim Christus aduenit,
sacerdotium Iudaeorum obmutuit, lex et prophetia cessauit.
Quartus Iohannes scripsit Euangelium ultimus in Asia, inci-
piens a Verbo, ut ostenderet eundem Saluatorem, qui pro no-
bis dignatus est nasci et pati, ipsum ante saecula Dei Verbum
esse, ipsum caelo uenisse, et post mortem ad caelum iterum
remeasse.

6. IN. Nunc uolo ut mihi exponas, quare quattuor sint qui
haec gesta conscripserunt? Seu etiam, qui sint hi quattuor, qui
diuino Spiritu adnuntiante propheta signati sunt?
RESP. Ideo ergo conscriptores <rerum> gestarum Euangelio-
rum quattuor esse dicuntur, quia, dicente Propheta, quattuor
animalia ostensa esse leguntur, quorum primum animal tenens
similitudinem hominis, secundum leonis, tertium uituli, quar-
tum uero aquilae. Sed hos quattuor has habentes figuras euan-
gelistas esse non / dubium est. 63r

7. IN. Isti euangelistae quare quattuor animalibus assimilati
sunt?
RESP. Quia per quattuor mundi partes fides Christianae reli-
gionis eorum praedicatione disseminata est.

8. IN. Quare dicuntur 'animalia'?
RESP. Quia propter animam hominis praedicatur Euangelium
Christi. Nam et oculis plena erant intus et foris, quoniam
praeuident Euangelia, quae dicta sunt a prophetis, et quae
promiserit in priori. Crura autem eorum recta, quia nihil prauum

1554–1555 *Fuit...Zacharias*: Lc 1:5
1558–1559 *Tu...Melchisedech*: Ps 109:4
1569–1574 This response is repeated at VII.12.
1571–1573 *quorum...aquilae*: see Ez 1:10

1553 initians: initiens *MS* **1554** *Iudaeae*: Iudae *MS* **1569** gestarum: gestae *MS*. **1573** hos: hi *MS* **1583** promiserit: promiserat *MS*

in Euangeliis repperitur, et alas habentes senas tegentes crura et facies suas: reuelata sunt enim quae tegebantur in aduentu Christi.

9. IN. Dic mihi cur euangelista in generatione Christi ordinem praeposterum posuisset, cum ante Dauid et postea nominauit Abraham?

RESP. Hic ordo in hoc loco necessitate est commutatus, quoniam si primum posuisset Abraham et postea Dauid, rursus ei repetendus erat Abraham, ut series generationis Christi texeretur.

10. IN. Quare ceteris praetermissis horum filium eum nuncupauit?

RESP. Ideo illum istorum filium esse dixit, quia ad hos tantum facta esse repromissio legitur.

11. IN. Qualiter promissio facta est ad Abraham, et qualiter / 63v
ad Dauid?

RESP. Abrahae dictum est: *In semine tuo benedicentur omnes gentes terrae*, quod est Christus. Dauid uero: *De fructu uentris tui ponam super sedem tuam.*

12. IN. Ordine primo Noui Testamenti finito, dic secundi ordinis qui sequitur auctores qui fuissent.

RESP. Prout intellego, dicam.

13. IN. Dic ergo, Epistolas Pauli quis scripsit et quot sunt, uel ubi et ubi leguntur scriptae?

RESP. Paulus apostolus suas scripsit Epistolas XIIII. Ex quibus nouem VII Ecclesiis scripsit; reliquas uero discipulis suis, Timotheo, Tito, et Filimoni. Ad Hebreos autem Epistola plerisque e Latinis eius esse incerta est propter dissonantiam sermonis, eamdemque alii Barnaban scripsisse, alii a Clemente scriptam fuisse suspicantur.

14. IN. Petri quis aut quot uel quomodo nominantur?

1587–1599 Questions 9 through 11 are repeated almost verbatin in VII.15–17 above.

1587–1705 The remainder of this chapter is considerably abridged from Isidore, *Prooemia* 92–109 (*PL* 83:176–180).

1600–1601 *In... terrae*: Gen 22:18

1601–1602 *De... tuam*: Ps 131:11

1610 Epistola: Epistolam *MS* **1611** e: a *MS*

RESP. Petrus scripsit duas nominis sui Epistolas, quae catholicae ideo nominantur, quia non uni tantum populo uel ciuitati sed uniuersis gentibus generaliter scriptae sunt.

15. IN. Iacobi, Iohannis et Iudae quis?

RESP. Iacob, Iohannes et Iudas suas scripserunt Epistolas.

16. IN. Actuum apostolorum scriptor quis extitit?

RESP. Actus apostolorum primordia fidei Christianae / in gen- 64r
tibus et nascentis Ecclesiae historiam digerit. Actuum apostolorum scriptorem Lucam esse euangelistam manifestum est, in quo opere nascentis Ecclesiae infantia texitur, et apostolorum historia retinetur. Vnde et Actus apostolorum dicitur.

17. IN. Apocalypsin quis aut quo tempore uel ubi?

RESP. Apocalipsin librum Iohannes euangelista scripsit eo tempore, quo ob Euangelii praedicationem in insula Pathmos traditur relegatus.

18. IN. Apocalipsis qua lingua dicitur uel quid interpretatur?

RESP. 'Apocalipsis' autem ex Greco, in Latinum 'reuelatio' interpretatur.

19. IN. Reuelatio quid est?

RESP. Reuelatio est manifestatio eorum quae abscondita erant, iuxta quod ipse Iohannes dicit: *Apocalipsis Iesu Christi, quem dedit illi Deus palam facere seruis suis.* Hi et ceteri, quos in Veteri Testamento paulo superius dinumerauimus, sunt scriptores sacrorum librorum per Spiritum Sanctum loquentes ad eruditionem nostram et praecepta uiuendi et credendi regulam conscripserunt. Praeter haec alia uolumina apocrifa nuncupantur.

20. IN. Quare dicuntur 'apocrifa'?

RESP. Apocrifa autem dicta, id est 'secreta,' quia in dubium
ueniunt. Est enim earum / occulta origo, nec patet Patribus, 64v
e quibus usque ad nos auctoritas ueracium Scripturarum certissima et notissima successione peruenit. In his apocrifis, etsi inuenitur aliqua ueritas, tamen propter multa falsa, nulla est in eis canonica auctoritas, quae recte a prudentibus iudicantur, non

1636–1637 *Apocalipsis…suis*: Apoc 1:1

1629 relegatus: religatus *MS*

esse eorum credenda, quibus adscribuntur. Nam multa et sub nominibus prophetarum et recentiora sub nominibus apostolorum ab hereticis proferuntur, quae omnia sub nomine apocriforum auctoritate canonica diligenti examinatione remota sunt.

21. IN. Ecce protulisti quadam ex parte interpretationes et numeros ordinesque atque scriptores, necnon et uocabula librorum Noui Testamenti; nunc peto ut quicquid in eis contineatur per singula currens breui sermone mihi exponas.
RESP. Nequaquam ab his, uolente Domino, lassabo.

22. IN. Dic ergo mihi, quid in libris Noui Testamenti principaliter contineatur?
RESP. Prout ille concedere dignatur, a quo et Vetus et Nouum exortum est Testamentum, iuxta quod nunc ratio exigit, dicam.

23. IN. Iam quia libri Euangeliorum in principio / illorum, 65r
sicut dignum est, positi sunt, dic mihi quid in eis habeatur.
RESP. Prout ualeo, in paucis tibi dicam. Continetur enim in illis praedicatio, quae tamen una esse dinoscitur, quia ex uno eodemque ore diuinitatis processit. Haec sunt enim quattuor flumina de uno Paradisi fonte manantia, quae per totum mundum caelestes praedicationes ministrant, et de fluento gratiae ac fidei uirorem infundunt.

24. IN. Quid continetur in Epistolis Pauli?
RESP. In illa quam scripsit ad Romanos fidem Romanae plebis conlaudat; in illis ad Corinthios geminam doctrinam castigat; ad Galatas per gratiam fidei excludit opera legis; ad Ephesios magnificat eos in fide quam acceperunt; ad Colosenses laudat eos pro eo quod [qui] in fide perstiterunt; ad Philipenses gratulatur eos Euangelium custodisse; ad Thesalonicenses fidem et operibus credidisse et persecutiones tolerasse eos gloriatur; ad Timotheum uero et Titum instruit Ecclesias; ad Philimonem rogat de Onesimo seruo emendato. In ultima uero quam scripsit / 65v
ad Hebreos, qui in Christo crediderant et postmodum persecutionibus iudaicis territi a fide recesserant, confortat atque ad gratiam Euangelii reuocat.

1673 *in illis…castigat*: see 1 Cor 1:10–4:21

1650 adscribuntur: adscribunt *MS* **1654** interpretationes: intemptationes *MS* **1669** fluento: fluenta *MS* **1676** perstiterunt: persteterunt *MS*

25. IN. Quid habetur in epistolis Petri?
RESP. Est enim ibi profunditas sensus, eo quod repleti sint sensibus, ut per eas diuinae scientiae sensus possint perscrutari.

26. IN. Quid in Iacobi?
RESP. Aedificatio Ecclesiae et infusio caritatis.

27. <IN. Quid in epistolis Iohannis?
RESP. In prima oficium caritatis> in amore Dei et fraterna dilectione. In secunda dilectionis studium hortatur. In tertia laus gagi in studio ueritatis et opera misericordiae uersatur.

28. IN. Quid in Iudae?
RESP. Increpatio blasphemantium in Christo.

29. IN. Quid in Actibus apostolorum?
RESP. Historia nascentis Ecclesiae et descriptio operis fidei.

30. IN. Quid in Apocalipsi?
RESP. Multa quidem et difficilia in eo leguntur, sed breuiter ex eo aliqua tibi proferam. Continetur enim in ipso filii hominis sedes in throno et XXIIII seniores, necnon et quattuor animalia praecedentia ante thronum, notaturque ibi finis mundi, pugna Michahelis cum dracone, interitus Antichristi, punitio diaboli, et ad ultimum resurrectio mortuorum, et nouitas caeli / ac terrae 66r
uel cetera. Haec pauca, frater, de Nouo Testamento ad praesens libenter suscipe, donec Deo uolente ex eo tibi maiora proferam.

<VII> DE GRADIBVS TOTIVS ECCLESIAE DIGNITATIS

1. IN. Dic ergo, frater, gradus ecclesiastici quot sunt?
RESP. De his, quae nunc temporis Deo uolente nobis conuenire possunt, octo sunt.

2. IN. Quomodo nominantur?
RESP. Primus ostiarius, secundus psalmista, tertius lector, quartus exorcista, quintus accolitus, sextus subdiaconus, septimus diaconus, octauus uero presbyter.

1692 *gagi*: an ersatz late form of vadium, 'wages.'
1712 *accolitus*: the acolyte is the highest of the minor orders (porter, psalmist, lector, exorcist, and acolyte). He was to be at least thirteen years old and his responsibilities involved serving as an assistant to the priest in the performance of his duties.
1711–1713 Taken from Isidore, *Etymologiae* 7.12.3.

1689–1690 IN…caritatis: *C; omitted from MS*

3. IN. Modo uolo ut dicas mihi quare dicitur 'ostiarius.' RESP. Secundum quod legi faciam. 'Hostiarii' dicti sunt, eo quod praesint hostiis templi, ut sciant recipere fideles et infideles respuere. Vnde et Dominus hostiarius dignatus est fieri, cum ostia inferni aperuit et electos suos inde abstulit, reprobos autem reliquit.

4. IN. Vnde uocatur 'psalmista'? RESP. Ab psalmis canendis. Ipsi enim canunt, ut excitent animas ad conpunctionem audientium.

5. IN. Quare dicuntur 'lectores'? RESP. Dicti sunt lectores a legendo. Illi enim praedicant populis, / quod sequantur. Vnde et Dominus lector dicitur, quando 66v
aperuit Dominus librum Isaiae prophetae et legit in medio plebis dicens: *Spiritus Domini super me, propter quod unxit me, euangelizare pauperibus misit me.*

6. IN. Quare dicitur 'exorcista'? RESP. 'Exorcistae' ex Greco in Latinum 'adiurantes' siue 'increpantes' uocantur. Vnde et Dominus exorcista fuit, quando septem daemonia de Maria Magdalenae eiecit.

7. IN. Vnde dicitur 'acolitus,' aut quale ministerium habet? RESP. 'Acoliti' Grece, Latine uero 'ceroferarii' dicuntur a 'deportandis cereis,' quando legendum est Euangelium et sacrificium offerendum.

8. IN. Quare uocatur 'subdiaconus'? RESP. Ideo 'subdiaconi' appellantur, quia subiacent praeceptis et officiis leuitarum. Oportet enim illis epistolam legere, honestare altare, et aquam praeparare in ministerio altaris. Vnde et Dominus subdiaconus est appellatus, quia in Cana Galileae aquam in uinum conuertit.

9. IN. Dic mihi, qua lingua dicitur 'diaconus,' aut unde dictus est 'diaconus'?

1715–1719 Taken from Isidore, *Etymologiae* 7.12.32.

1727–1728 *Spiritus... me*: Is 61:1; Lc 4:18. Cf. Isidore, *Etymologiae* 7.12.24. On the casting out of Mary Magdalene's demons, see Lc 8:2 and Mc 16:9.

1730–1732 Taken from Isidore, *Etymologiae* 7.12.31.

1734–1736 Taken from Isidore, *Etymologiae* 7.12.29.

1735 cereis: caereis *MS* **1739** epistolam: apostolum *MS*

RESP. 'Diaconus' enim Grece, Latine 'minister' dicitur, quia sicut in sacerdote consecratio, ita et in diacono ministerii
dispensatio habetur. Vnde et Dominus diaconus / dictus est, 67r
quando lauit pedes discipulorum suorum.

10. IN. Vnde idem diaconus 'Leuita' appellatur?
RESP. 'Leuitae' ex nomine auctoris uocati. De Leui enim Leuitae exorti sunt.

11. IN. Iam quia de diaconibus ac leuitis, quorum ministerium proprium est Euangelium legere, nunc ratio instat; uolo ut dicas mihi, quid sit Euangelium aut unde descendit uel cuius in eo uerba ponuntur?
RESP. Euangelium dicitur proprie bona adnuntiatio, quae utique adnuntiatio est Domini nostri Iesu Christi, et uitam adnuntiat post mortem. Descendit autem Euangelium ab eo quem adnuntiet et ostendat, quod is, qui per prophetas suos loquebatur, uenit in carne, sicut scriptum est: *Qui loquebar, ecce adsum.*

12. IN. Explicasti autem quid sit Euangelium, uel unde descendat, nunc obsecro, ut mihi aperies, quare quattuor sint, qui haec gesta scripserunt, seu etiam qui sunt hi quattuor, qui uno spiritu adnuntiante Propheta signati sunt?
RESP. Ideo ergo conscriptores <rerum> gestarum Euangeliorum quattuor esse dicuntur, quia, dicente Propheta, quattuor animalia ostensa esse leguntur, quorum primum animal tenens
similitudinem hominis, secundum leonis, tertium uituli, quar-
tum / uero aquilae. Sed hos quattuor has habentes figuras eu- 67v
angelistas esse non dubium est.

13. IN. Ecce dixisti numerum et figuras singulorum, modo uolo ut dicas omnium illorum nomina, seu etiam et ob quam rationem singuli illorum has uideantur obtinere figuras?
RESP. Nomina eorum haec sunt: Matheus, Marcus, Lucas, Iohannes. Sed ut quid has figuras obtineant, Domino miserante, exponam.

1750–1751 Taken from Isidore, *Etymologiae* 7.12.22.
1753 *legere*: supply 'dixisti' here in order to provide the sentence with a main verb.
1760 *Qui...adsum*: Is 52:6
1765–1770 This response is repeated from VI.6.

1758 quem: quo *MS* **1765** gestarum: gestae *MS* **1769** hos: hi *MS*

14. IN. Fac.

RESP. Mattheus idcirco figuram hominis in se habet, qui ab initio Euangelii sui generationem et natiuitatem Saluatoris enarret. Sic enim incipit: *Liber generationis Iesu Christi*, et cetera. Marcus leonis gerens figuram, quia a solitudine incipit dicens: *Vox clamantis in deserto: Parate uiam Domini*. Lucas uituli speciem gestat, ad cuius similitudinem Saluator noster est immolatus, et ideo Lucas uitulo conparatur, quia duo cornua duo Testamenta, et quattuor pedum ungulas quattuor Euangelia designantur, et quia eo tempore uituli in sacrificio offerebantur. Sic enim a sacerdotibus incipit: *Fuit in diebus Herodis regis sacerdos quidam nomine Zacharias de uice Abia et uxor eius de filiabus Aaron, nomen Elisabeth*. Iohannes habet / similitudinem 68r
aquilae, eo quod alta petiit. Ait enim: *In principio erat Verbum, et Verbum erat apud Deum, et Deus erat Verbum; hoc erat in principio apud Deum*. Et Dauid dicit de persona Christi: *Renouabitur sicut aquilae iuuentus tua*, id est Christi Iesu Domini nostri, quia resurgens a mortuis ascendit ad caelos.

15. IN. Frater, prout potui, solui tibi quaestionem tuam, rogo, si placet, ut dicas mihi cur euangelista in generatione Christi ordinem praeposterum posuisset, cum ante Dauid et postea nominauit Abraham?

RESP. Vere secundum quod legendo didici, referam. Hic ordo in hoc loco necessitate est commutatus. Si enim primum posuisset Abraham et postea Dauid, rursus ei repetendus esset Abraham, ut generationis series texeretur.

16. IN. Quare ceteris praetermissis horum filium eum nuncupauit?

RESP. Ideo illum istorum filium esse dixerunt, quia ad hos tantum facta esse repromissio legitur.

17. IN. Qualiter promissio facta est ad Abraham, et qualiter ad Dauid?

1780 *Liber…Christi*: Mt 1:1
1782 *Vox…Domini*: Mc 1:3
1787–1789 *Fuit…Elisabeth*: Lc 1:5
1790–1792 *In…Deum*: Io 1:1
1792–1793 *Renouabitur…tua*: Ps 102:5
1795–1811 Questions 15 through 17 are repeated almost verbatim from their previous occurrence in VI.9–11.

RESP. Abrahae dictum est: *In semine tuo benedicentur omnes gentes terrae*, quod est Christus. Dauid uero: / *De fructu uentris* 68v *tui ponam super sedem tuam.*

18. <IN.> Haec pauca propter breuitatem diei de ratione Euangeliorum conscriptorumque suorum, si placet dominationi uestrae, hac uice sufficere possunt. Nunc ad cetera transeamus.

RESP. Fiat, ut dicis.

19. IN. Dic mihi, 'presbyter' qua lingua uocatur, et unde est appellatus?

RESP. 'Presbyter' Grece, Latine 'senior' interpretatur; non tamen propter aetatem uel decrepitam senectutem, sed propter honorem et dignitatem, quam acceperunt, ita uocantur.

20. IN. Quare idem 'sacerdos' appellatur?

RESP. 'Sacerdos' enim nomen conpositum habet ex Greco et Latino, quasi 'sacrum dans.' Quoniam sicut 'rex' a 'regendo,' ita 'sacerdos' a 'sanctificando' uocatus est. Consecrat enim et sanctificat.

21. IN. Ecce, frater mi, de ratione graduum, de quibus interrogasti, rationem tibi in paucis deduxi. Nunc peto ut rationem missae, quae ab illis celebratur, quare uocetur, mihi exponas.

RESP. Certe, frater, difficilem rem a me requires. Sed tamen prout nunc ratio exigit, secundum quod scio, tibi respondere non negabo.

22. IN. Vnde dicta est 'missa'?

RESP. Ab 'emittendo.'

23. IN. Qua ratione?

RESP. Missa / enim tempore sacrificii est, quando catecumini 69r foras mittebantur clamante leuita: Si quis catecuminus remansit, foras mittatur, quia sacramentis altaris interesse non possunt, qui nondum regenerati noscuntur.

24. IN. Hoc 'sacrificium,' quod dixisti, quare ita est appellatum?

1809–1810 *In…terrae*: Gen 22:18
1810–1811 *De…tuam*: Ps 131:11
1818–1820 Taken from Isidore, *Etymologiae* 7.12.20.
1822–1825 Taken from Isidore, *Etymologiae* 7.12.17.
1835–1838 Taken from Isidore, *Etymologiae* 6.19.4.

1814 possunt: potest *MS* **1837** sacramentis: sacramenta *MS*

RESP. 'Sacrificium' est dictum, eo quod sit sacrum factum, quod prece mystica consecratur pro nobis in memoriam Dominicae passionis. Vnde et eo iubente hoc corpus et sanguinem Christi dicimus, quod ut sit ex fructibus terrae sanctificatum, et fit sacramentum operante inuisibiliter Spiritu Dei. Cuius panis et calicis sacramentum Greci 'Eucharistiam' dicunt, quod Latine 'bona gratia' interpretatur.

25. IN. 'Offertorium' unde uocatur?

RESP. 'Offertorium' dicitur 'oblatio,' eo quod altaribus fertur et sanctificatur a sacerdotibus.

26. IN. Inter 'dona' et 'munera' quid interest?

RESP. 'Dona' proprie 'Dei' dicuntur; 'munera' hominum sunt.

27. IN. Qua ratione?

RESP. Munera enim dicuntur obsequia, quae pauperes loco munerum diuitibus soluunt; donum autem, quod Deo datur. Vnde et in templis 'donaria' dicimus.

28. IN. / 'Munera' unde uocantur? 69v

RESP. Dicuntur 'munera,' eo quod manibus uel accipiantur uel dantur.

29. IN. Quot sunt, quae offeruntur?

RESP. Duo.

30. IN. Quae?

RESP. Donum et sacrificium.

31. IN. Quid est donum?

RESP. Donum est, quicquid auro argentoque aut qualibet alia specie efficitur.

32. IN. Quid est sacrificium?

RESP. Sacrificium est uictima et quaecumque in ara cremantur seu ponuntur. Quia omne, quod Deo datur, aut dicatur aut consecratur.

33. IN. Qua ratione?

RESP. Quod enim dicatur, dicendo datur, unde et appellatur.

1841–1847 Taken from Isidore, *Etymologiae* 6.19.38.
1849–1850 Taken from Isidore, *Etymologiae* 6.19.24.
1851–1903 Questions 26 through 39 paraphrase, in order, Isidore, *Etymologiae* 6.19.26–38.

1842 quod: quia *MS* **1852** Dei: diuinae *MS* **1855** loco: locum *MS*

Vnde errant, qui consecrationem dedicationem putant significari.

34. IN. 'Immolatio' unde dicitur?

RESP. 'Immolatio' ab 'antiquis' est dicta, eo quod in mole altaris uictimae cederentur. Vnde et 'mactatio' post 'immolationem.' Nunc autem immolatio panis et calicis conuenit.

35. IN. Quid est libatio?

RESP. Libatio tantummodo calicis est oblatio. Vnde dicitur: *Et libauit de sanguine uuae*; nam libare fundere est.

36. IN. 'Hostiae' unde uocantur?

RESP. 'Hostiae' apud ueteres dicebantur 'sacrificia,' quae fiebant antequam ad hostem pergerent.

37. IN. Quid sunt 'uictimae,' aut quare ita / uocantur? 70r

RESP. 'Victimae' dicuntur 'sacrificia,' quae post uictoriam de uictis hostibus immolabant. Et erant uictimae maiora sacrificia quam hostia. Alii uictimam dictam putauerunt, quia ictu percussa cadebat, uel quia uincta ad aras ducebatur.

38. IN. 'Holocaustum' unde uocatur?

RESP. Holocaustum est, ubi totum igne consumitur, quod offertur. *Holo* enim Grece totum dicitur, <*kausis* incensio>: unde et 'holocaustum,' 'totum incensum.'

39. IN. Quid sunt caerimoniae?

RESP. Caerimoniae apud Latinos dicuntur 'sacra' omnia, quae apud Grecos 'orgia' uocantur. Proprie autem uisum est doctoribus a 'carendo' appellari 'caerimonia,' quasi 'cerimonias,' eo quod ea, quae in sacris diuinis offeruntur, in suo usu id carerent homines. Alii caerimonias proprie in obseruationibus Iudaeorum credunt, abstinentiam scilicet quarundam escarum

1881–1882 *Et…uuae*: Eccl 50:16

1893 *Holo*: Latinization of the Greek Ὅλον.

1898 *Caerimonia* here is not meant to signify 'ceremonia' directly, but to serve as a bridge-word illustrating what Isidore thinks to be the etymological link between 'carendo' and 'ceremonia.'

1899–1900 *quae…homines*: 'whatever is offered in holy rituals, men do without for their own use.'

1896–1903 *Caerimoniae…abstinuerunt*: Isidore, *Etymologiae* 6.19.36–37. After this entry, the text abandons the *Etymologiae* as its source.

1877 mole: mola *MS* **1893** <*kausis* incensio>: *Isidore*. Kausis *is a Latinization of the Greek* καῦσις. **1900** proprie: propria *MS*

secundum ueterem legem, eo quod obseruantes careant his rebus quibus se abstinuerint.

40. IN. Ipsa missa a quo pontifice sumpsit initium?
RESP. Ordo autem missae uel orationum, quibus oblata Deo sacrificia consecrantur, primo a sancto Petro est insti / tutus, 70v
cuius celebratione uno eodemque uocabulo uniuersus peragit orbis.

41. IN. Obsecro humiliter, quid in eadem missa contineatur, ut mihi aperire non dedigneris.
RESP. Prout intellego dicam. In ordine totius missae septem orationes continentur.

42. IN. Quae sunt haec?
RESP. Prima earundem oratio, ubi dicitur 'Dominus uobiscum' uel 'Oremus,' ammonitio est erga populum, ut excitentur ad Deum adorandum. Secunda quidem collecta, quae posthaec sequitur, inuocatio est ad Deum, ut clementer suscipiat preces fidelium et oblationes eorum. Tertia autem effunditur oratio pro offerentibus siue pro defunctis fidelibus in collecta, quae dicitur post sacrificii receptionem, ut per eundem sacrificium ueniam consequi mereantur. Quarta, quae posthaec infertur pro osculo pacis et caritate reconciliationis a 'sursum corda' usque 'per Christum Dominum nostrum.' Quinta deinde ponitur inlatio in sanctificatione oblationis, a loco, ubi dicitur: 'Per quem maiestatem tuam laudant angeli,' usque ad eum locum, ubi 'osanna in excelsis' cantatur. In qua / etiam ad laudem terrestrium crea- 71r
turarum, uirtutumque caelestium uniuersitas prouocatur. Porro sexta exhinc succedit: 'Te igitur, clementissime Pater,' quae est confirmatio sacramenti; ut oblatio sanctificata per Spiritum Sanctum, corpori, ac sanguini conformetur. Septima uero oratio est, quam Dominus noster discipulis suis instituit orare dicens: 'Pater noster, qui es in caelis.'

43. IN. Dic mihi in hac oratione quot petitiones habentur?
RESP. Ego respondi tibi in paucis, prout noui, rationem missae.

1904–1961 The source for the remaining questions of this chapter (40–47) is Isidore, *De ecclesiasticis officiis* XV (*PL* 83:752–753).

1914–1932 The prayers mentioned form parts of the liturgy of the early medieval office.

1929 ut: et *MS* **1930** corpori, ac sanguini: corpus ac sanguinem *MS (The emended text follows the parallel passage in Isidore.)*

44. IN. Nunc obsecro, ut mihi similiter, prout intellegis, quid in ista oratione contineatur, dicere non abneges.
RESP. Prout intellego, faciam. In hac oratione septem petitiones continentur.

45. IN. Quae sunt hae?
RESP. Prima est: 'Pater noster, qui es in caelis, sanctificetur nomen tuum.' Secunda: 'Adueniat regnum tuum.' Tertia: 'Fiat uoluntas tua, sicut in caelo et in terra.' Quarta: 'Panem nostrum cotidianum da nobis hodie.' Quinta: 'Et dimitte nobis debita nostra, sicut et nos dimittimus debitoribus nostris.' Sexta: 'Et ne nos inducas in temptationem.' Septima: 'Sed libera nos a malo.' Halleluia. / 71v

46. IN. Nunc obsecro, ut dicas mihi, quid in isdem petitionibus contineatur?
RESP. In tribus primis aeterna poscuntur, in sequentibus quattuor temporalia, quae tamen propter aeterna adipiscenda petuntur.

47. IN. Quomodo?
RESP. Nam cum dicimus: 'Sanctificetur nomen tuum. Adueniat regnum tuum. Fiat uoluntas tua, sicut in caelo et in terra,' hic quidem ista tria inchoantur, sed in illa uita sperantur, ubi sanctificatio Dei et uoluntas et regnum in sanctis suis inmortaliter permanebit. Iam uero panis cotidianus, qui uel animae uel carni tribuitur, hic exposcitur. Hic post omnia, ut a malis liberemur, Dei auxilium imploramus. In tribus autem, quae superius dixi, nihil horum est. Hanc itaque orationem Saluator discipulos suos docuit, in qua spes continetur fidelium et confessio peccatorum.

<VIII> INCIPIT DE FIDE

1. IN. Ista suscipio. Sed quoniam, sicut nosti, omnes per fidem saluari credimus, rogo ut dicas mihi, quomodo fidem tuam intellegis, uel etiam in quem credis?

1940–1946 *Pater noster…malo*: Mt 6:9–13 (the Lord's Prayer)

1963–2043 No source has been identified for questions 1–19. However, the whole of the first 19 questions is reproduced nearly exactly as the second part of the *Commentarius in orationem dominicam, symbolum apostolorim et fidem athanasii* of Bruno Herbipolensis. Bruno (Bishop of Würzburg 1034–1045, d. 1045) a cousin of Emperor Conrad II, served as an adviser to him and his successor, Henry III, and also held the position of Imperial

RESP. Ego credo in Deum Patrem omnipotentem, creatorem caeli et terrae.

2. IN. Quare dicitur 'omnipotens,' et quare / 'creator'? 72r

RESP. 'Omnipotens' dicitur, quia omnia potest; 'creator,' eo quod omnia creauit, caelum, terram, mare, et omnia quae in eis sunt.

3. IN. Credis in Iesum Christum?

RESP. Omnino credo in Iesum Christum Filium eius unicum Dominum nostrum, qui est uerus Deus et uerus homo.

4. IN. Quomodo Deus, et quomodo uerus est homo?

RESP. Deus uerus est, quia de Spiritu Sancto conceptus est. Homo uerus est, quia ex Maria Virgine natus est.

5. IN. Ecce illum natum. Quid postea factum est?

RESP. Post sanctam enim eius natiuitatem aetate et sapientia crescens XXX annos impleuit. In qua etiam aetate a Ioanne Baptista dignatus est baptizari, et post baptismum tribus annis et dimidio docuit et praedicauit omnia, quae ad uitam aeternam pertinent.

6. IN. Post hanc praedicationem quid factum est?

RESP. In ipsa praedicatione conpraehensus est ab iniquis et perfidis Iudaeis, a quibus propter inuidiam illorum et propter peccata nostra multa blasphemia multasque passiones sub Pontio Pilato, qui iudex erat illo tempore in Iudea, sustinuit.

7. IN. Vnde dicitur 'Pontius'? / 72v

RESP. A loco, ubi natus fuit, hoc nomen accepit.

8. IN. Quid post haec?

RESP. Sub illo enim crucifixus est, et in eadem cruce mortuus. Deinde sepultus est, et, manente corpore in sepulchro, anima eius ad inferna descendit. De quo inferno sanctos patriarchas, id sunt Abraham, Isaac et Iacob, et sanctos prophetas, Esaiam, Hieremiam, et reliquos, ac ceteros omnes, quos elegit, misericorditer liberauit, et uictor tertia die a mortuis resurrexit.

Chancellor of Italy from 1027–1034. He then became bishop of Würzburg, where he left his mark in education and church restoration. His exegesis of the Psalms and his catechetical writings are edited in *PL* 142:39–568. The second part of the commentary, *symbolum apostolorum*, occurs on col. 559–561. Given that each of the surviving MSS of the *Disputatio* originates from the regions surrounding Würzburg, it is likely that it served as Bruno's primary source.

9. IN. Postquam resurrexit, quid fecit?

RESP. Post nobilissimam enim et sanctissimam eius resurrectionem conuersatus est XL diebus et XL noctibus cum discipulis suis, et manducauit cum illis, multa docens et loquens de regno Dei.

10. IN. Quid postea?

RESP. Post haec uero uidentibus illis ascendit in caelum, ubi quomodo uult et qualiter uult, sedet ad dexteram Dei Patris omnipotentis.

11. IN. Quid posthaec facturus erit?

RESP. Finito mundi termino cum ipso corpore, cum quo ascendit in caelum, uenturus est iudicare uiuos et mortuos.

12. IN. Qui sunt uiui et qui sunt mortui?

RESP. Viui iusti; mortui peccatores.

13. IN. Credis in Spiritum / Sanctum? 73r

RESP. Credo sine dubio in Spiritum Sanctum, quidem Deus est et in Trinitate tertia persona, quia alia est persona Patris, alia Filii, alia Spiritus Sancti. In qua Trinitate unum Deum omnino esse credo et confiteor.

14. IN. Credis in sanctam Ecclesiam catholicam et in sanctorum communionem?

RESP. Esse etenim sanctam Ecclesiam sed non in illam credo, quia non Deus, sed conuocatio seu congregatio Christianorum <est> sicut superius dixi.

15. IN. Quid est 'catholica'?

RESP. Vniuersalis, id est per totum orbem diffusa. Sanctorum communionem, id est cum sanctis societatem et communionem habere credo, si fidem firmiter tenuero et operibus seruauero.

16. IN. 'Ecclesia' qua lingua dicitur?

RESP. Greca.

17. IN. Quid interpretatur Latine?

RESP. 'Conuocatio' seu 'congregatio Christianorum,' sicut superius dixi.

18. IN. Credis in remissionem peccatorum?

RESP. Non, sed esse remissionem peccatorum credo, quia propter hoc dignatus est Dei Filius carnem adsumere, ut nos, qui propter peccata nostra salui esse non poteramus, eius misericordia saluaremur.

19. IN. Credis in carnis resurrec/tionem? 73v

RESP. Non credo in illam, sed carnem, quam in hac uita sub mortali conditione portamus, resurrecturam esse inmortalem credo, et pro consortio animae rationem reddituram. Vitam aeternam uero sine dubio nos consequuturos credamus, si ista, quae hucusque exposuimus, firmiter teneamus, et operibus fideliter impleamus.

20. SI EIVSDEM FIDEI RATIONEM PLENIVS NOSSE DESIDERAS, IN ORDINE SEQVENTI INVENIES.

21. IN. Dic mihi, 'symbolum' in quo haec eadem fides continetur, cuius lingua uocatur, et quo tempore, uel a quibus auctoribus sit conpositum. Seu etiam, qui illud conposuerunt, quorum sint exemplum consecuti?

RESP. Certe, frater, cum scias me paruum non solum corpore sed et sensu, ualde difficilem rationem a me requiris, sed tamen propter eiusdem fidei dilectionem ea, quae de illa Dominus mihi administrare dignatur, tibi pandere non denegabo.

22. IN. Nisi enim tuam dilectionem talem cognoscerem, nequaquam talia a te requirere debuissem.

RESP. 'Symbolum' namque nomen est Grecum, quod Latine 'conlatio pecuniae' interpretatur, quod et beati apostoli post susceptionem Spiritus Sancti, / priusquam ab inuicem sepa- 74r
rarentur, pro signo fidei conposuerunt. Sed quorum exemplum in hoc facto fuissent imitati, secundum quod legi, breuiter ostendam. Quaedam Israheliticae tribus cum aduersum se ciuili proelio decertarent, et propter unius populi <arma> uel habitum

2038–2040 *Non credo… reddituram*: it is unclear why the author would draw this distinction.

2044–2045 *SI… INVENIES*: The capitalization occurs in the manuscript.

2046–2303 The source for the rest of the chapter is pseudo-Maximus' *Homily LXXXIII: De traditione Symboli*, edited in *PL* 57:431–440. The author follows the same method as he did with Isidore, which is to rework excerpted passages from his source into question-and-answer dialogue. In contrast to his revisions of Isidore, however, the author alters the homily more freely, both adding and deleting much more than he does elsewhere. The names of the author of each verse (Andreas, Jacobus, etc.) have all been added, and the discussion of each verse has been expanded beyond that found in pseudo-Maximus.

2061 ciuili *B*: ciuibus *MS*

inter bellantes discretio esse non possit, tribus illa, cuius iustior erat causa pugnandi, et per Dei auxilium uictoriam se habere putabat, signaculum sibi certo in sermone constituit, ut quos unius habitus et una armorum similitudo confuderat, secretioris uerbi distingueret sacramentum. Quod et beati apostoli, qui Ecclesiam Dei contra malitiam diabolici furoris armabant, et defensores ac propugnatores illius erant futuri, hoc sequentes exemplum mysterium symboli tradiderunt. Et quia sub uno nomine Christi credentium erat futura diuersitas, signaculum symboli inter fideles perfidosque secerneret, quis fidelis quisue hostis appareret Ecclesiae.

23. IN. Valde placent quae dicis, si tamen nomina illarum tribuum, nomenque secreti sermonis, de quo dixeras, indicare uoluisses.

RESP. Si rite recordor, faciam, quod petisti. Cum Iepte
dux / iustioris tribus Galaad cognouisset inimicos eius, tribus 74v
uidelicet Effraim, aduersum se aduenisse, occupauit continuo uada Iordanis, per quae illi reuerti debuerant. Qui dum se superatos cognoscerent, et de praelio fugientes per eadem uada euadere uolentes transeundi licentiam postolabant, interrogabaturque eos: 'Vnde estis'? Qui respondentes, 'de Galaad.' Statimque illis dicebatur: 'Si de Galaad estis, dicite ergo 'Seboleth,' quod interpretatur spica.' Quod cum dicere non poterant, protinus capite truncabantur, ut secreti sermonis ueritas probaretur. Hic est enim sermo secretus, quem Galaditides sibi pro signo constituerunt. Ad cuius similitudinem, nisi fallor, praefatum symbolum beati apostoli conscripserunt, ut inter fideles et infideles Ecclesiae, sicut superius dictum est, ueritatem credulitatis discernere potuissent incipiente beato Petro apostolo, qui ait: 'Credo in Deum Patrem omnipotentem,' et cetera.

24. IN. Optima sunt ualde, quae dicis. Sed obsecro, ut quomodo aut qualiter uel in quem credere debeam, diligenter aperias.

2077–2088 *Cum…constituerunt*: This passage paraphrases Iud 12:4–6.
2092 *Credo…omnipotentem*: the first verse of the Apostles' Creed.

2066 confuderat: confunderat *MS*

RESP. Iuxta quod intellego, faciam. Credendus est sine dubio Deus Pater omnipotens, cuius sic uirtus / 75r sentitur, ut quantitas eius et qualitas ignoretur. Esse enim illius et posse non discutiendo adsequimur, sed credendo. In quem autem credere debeamus, edocet nos redemptoris nostri auctoritas dicens: *Qui credit in me et in eum qui me misit, habet uitam aeternam.* Et alibi: *Credite in Deum, et in me credite.* Plus enim, frater, mihi est, quod fidei oculis uidemus, quam sensus noster carnalis possit conspicere.

25. IN. Credo omnino, sicut dicis. Sed peto ut dicas quid in Deo, quid in Patre, quidue in omnipotente debeam intellegere?

RESP. In Deo siquidem natura innascibilis, in Patre unigeniti ueritas, in omnipotente uero plenitudo uirtutis ostenditur.

26. IN. Quomodo?

RESP. Est namque per ingenitam deitatem omnipotens, et per omnipotentiam Pater. Non enim inquirere debemus qualiter sit Pater, quia qualiter Deus sit aut omnipotens non potest humanis mentibus conpraehendi.

27. IN. Ratio, quam de primo uersu protulisti, hac uice sufficere potest. Sed quis secundum conposuisset, uel qualiter eum intellegere debeam, innotesce.

RESP. Andreas secundum uersum conposuit dicens: 'Et in Iesum Christum Filium eius unicum Dominum nostrum.' / 75v Sicut enim Patrem rerum omnium Deum, ita oportet nos et Filium eius Dominum nostrum Iesum Christum, qui est Verbum ipsius, confiteri, cuius principium ex ipso est, quia Deus Verbum est. Quod autem Christus est factus, qui Filius erat, dispensatio est redemptionis humanae. Quod uero Dominus est, de proprietate naturae est. Vnicus siquidem uel unigenitus adnuntiatur et creditur, quia unus ita est genitus, neque habet in unitate consortem. Filium audis, non ut illum aliquo sexu editum putes, sed ut credas inconpraehensibili maiestate Deum

2099 *Esse…posse*: infinitives used as substantives here.
2101–2102 *Qui…aeternam*: Io 3:15
2103 *Credite…credite*: Io 14:1
2119–2120 *Et…nostrum*: the second verse of the Apostles' Creed.

2127 habet: libet *MS*

prodisse de Deo, ut ipse ait: *Ego a Patre exiui et ueni in hunc mundum.*

28. IN. Tertium uersum quis conposuit, aut quid in eo intellegitur?

RESP. Iacobus ait: 'Qui conceptus est de Spiritu Sancto natus ex Maria Virgine.' Spiritum Deum esse Saluator ipse nos docuit dicens in Euangelio: *Quia Spiritus Deus est.* Et ideo natum Christum de Spiritu Sancto et Maria Virgine confitemur. Spiritum Sanctum audis, ut partum illum mirabilem simul et inculpabilem recognoscas. Quoniam caeleste est quod Spiritus agit, et inuiolatum quod sanctus operatur. Nam / cum unigenitum 76r
Dei hominem fieri redemptionis nostrae necessitas flagitaret, hoc natiuitatis suae priuilegium propriae diuinitati inuexit, ut de uirgine nasceretur. Qui enim ueniebat inueteratam peccatis hominum renouare naturam, nouam legem uoluit habere nascendi. Vnigenitus igitur Dei factus est filius hominis, ut qui erat mundi creator, fieret, et redemptor.

29. IN. Quarti uersus conpositorem, siue quid in eo contineatur, expone.

RESP. Beatus Iohannes apostolus quartum conposuit uersum, dicens: 'Passus sub Pontio Pilato, crucifixus, mortuus, et sepultus.' Iste Pilatus iudex erat illo tempore in Iudea a Tiberio Caesare constitutus, sub quo Dominus passus est, qui etiam 'Pontius' a loco, unde natus est, appellatur. Hunc itaque Dominum nostrum Iesum Christum sicut perfectum Deum, ita et perfectum hominem confiteri debemus. De cuius cruce nulla sit nobis confusio, quia habemus de eius passione uictoriam. Sicut enim Dei Filius non sibi sed nobis natus est, inmaculatus Dei Agnus non sibi sed nobis est passus. Quis autem non mirum aduertat / 76v
esse mysterium, ubi ipse praedicatur, qui Deus est, et ubi Dominus adnuntiatur, qui adseritur crucifixus? Nam crucem illam, in qua confixus est corpore, nos gestamus in fronte. Et ideo inlusiones et obprobria, mortemque, quam sustinuit, non debemus

2130–2131 *Ego…mundum*: Io 16:28
2134–2135 *Qui…Virgine*: the third verse of the Apostles' Creed.
2136 *Quia…est*: Io 4:24
2150–2151 *Passus…sepultus*: the fourth verse of the Apostles' Creed.

2142 diuinitati: diuinitatis *MS*

suspiriis ingemescere sed continuis laudibus celebrare, quoniam satis abundeque gloriam passionis eius ostenderunt repentina obscuritas solis, tremor terrarum, saxorum diuisio, et resurrectio mortuorum. Sepultus est autem, quia consequens erat, ut qui mortuus fuerat, acciperet sepulturam. Qualiter ad consolationem sepultorum benedictionem corporis eius terra susciperet, ut qui uere mortuus cernebatur, uere a mortuis redisse crederetur.

30. IN. Quinti uersus conpositorem eiusque explanationem a te audire desidero.

RESP. Philippus quintum uersum exposuit dicens: 'Descendit ad inferna, tertia die resurrexit a mortuis.' In hoc enim Trinitatis mysterium et naturalis legis ostenditur resolutio, ut hominem in inferno positum eleuaret / ad caelum. 77r Decebat enim ut mors, quae per hominem subintrauerat, per hominem solueretur. Et sicut credimus, quod mortis est, ita utique credamus, quod uitae est. Et sicut in passione mysterium est pietatis, ita in resurrectione operatio potestatis, sicut ipse ait: *Potestatem habeo ponendi animam meam, et potestatem habeo iterum sumendi eam.* Quis enim stultus non credat illum resurrexisse, ad cuius praeceptum Lazarus sepultus est emersus de tumulo?

31. IN. Sextum uersum quis conposuit, aut quid in eo est intellegendum?

RESP. Bartholomeus sextum uersum ita conposuit, dicens: 'Ascendit in caelum.' Illuc enim ascendit, unde uenerat; non tamen alicuius iussione, sed propria uoluntate. Decebat enim talis gloria hominem, qui de uirgine nascebatur. Nec fuit ei inpossibile caelum ascendere, cui possibile fuit inferos triumphare. Et ideo necesse erat, ut qui ad mortem de regno uenerat, post mortem rediret ad regnum. Et sicut terra laetata est Dei Filium se suscepisse, ita caelum filium hominis se accepisse gauderet, dicente Propheta: / *Laetentur caeli et exultet terra.* 77v

2173–2174 *Descendit...mortuis*: the fifth verse of the Apostles' Creed.
2181–2182 *Potestatem...eam*: Io 10:18
2187–2188 *Ascendit in caelum*: the sixth verse of the Apostles' Creed.
2195 *Laetentur...terra*: Ps 95:11

2180 potestatis: pietatis *MS* **2183** ad: aut *MS*

32. IN. Septimi uersus auctorem, eiusque intellectum ut mihi exponas, obsecro.
RESP. Thomas septimi uersus auctor exstitit dicens: ‘Sedet ad dexteram Dei Patris omnipotentis.’ Quod sedet, Christi uictoriae munus est; quod ad dexteram Patris sedet, diuinitatis est priuilegium et consortium indiscretae caritatis, ut ostenderet locum iustis et sinistram peccatoribus demonstraret. Bene enim ad dexteram Patris adnuntiatur sedere, in quo nihil uoluntatis suae diabolus, qui totus est sinister, inuenit.

33. IN. Octauum uersum quis fecit, aut quid in eo continetur?
RESP. Mattheus octauum uersum conponens ait: ‘Inde uenturus est iudicare uiuos et mortuos.’ In ipso enim corpore Dominus uenturus est ad iudicium, in quo ascendit ad caelum. Necesse est quidem, ut genus humanum ille discutiat, qui creauit; et ipse iudicet, qui redemit. Iustum quippe est, ut omnipotens Dominus mortales suos, quos uirtute diuinitatis formauit, Patris pietate saluauit, iudicis examinatione discernat, ut impios gehennae ignis tradat, pios autem in societate / aeternitatis adsumat. Quid 78r
namque iustius potest esse apud Deum, quam ut quorum uita diuersa fuit in saeculo, eorum post hoc saeculum merita distinguantur. Vbi autem iudicandi referuntur <uiui> ac mortui, ibi omnium hominum esse apud Deum cura credatur.

34. IN. Nonum uersum quis conposuit, aut quomodo est intellegendus?
RESP. Item Iacobus nonum uersum adiungens ait: ‘Credo in Spiritum Sanctum.’ Hoc ad formam fidei pertinet, ut sicut in Patrem et Filium, ita et in Spiritum Sanctum absque ulla dubitatione credamus; ut quorum unum nomen est, non sit eorum diuersa confessio. Et qui in caelo apud se unum sunt, a nobis non separentur in terris, quoniam sicut diuinitati nihil de creaturis aequari potest, ita omnem diuisionem et inaequalitatem natura diuinitatis excludit. Itaque secundum euangelicam ueritatem, sicut Filius a Patre exiuit, ita et Spiritus Sanctus a Patre procedit. Et sicut unigenitus Filius Dei est, ita et Spiritus

2198–2199 *Sedet…omnipotentis*: the seventh verse of the Apostles’ Creed.
2207–2208 *Inde…mortuos*: the eighth verse of the Apostles’ Creed.
2221–2222 *Credo…Sanctum*: the ninth verse of the Apostles’ Creed.

Sanctus Dei est. Et sicut Pater, cui uult, miseretur, et Filius, cui uult, Patrem reuelat, ita etiam Spiritus et inspirare legitur, prout uult, et dona caelestium gratiarum diuidere, prout uult. / 78v
Quae cum ita se habeant, quomodo non unum esse cum Patre Filioque credendus est Spiritus, cui aequaliter adiacet posse quod uult?

35. IN. Omnino credendum est ita, ut adseris. Sed peto, ut decimi uersus auctorem, eiusque intellectum mihi exponas.

RESP. Simon decimi uersus auctor exstitit dicens: 'Sanctam Ecclesiam catholicam,' et cetera. Esse etenim sanctam Ecclesiam, sed non in eam credere debemus, quia non Deus, sed populus et domus est Dei, per quam et sanctificatio data est mortalibus, et crescente credentium numero omnium pene linguis in Dei laudibus sanctior mundus exultat. Quae etiam baptismi sacramento, peccatorum contaminatione detersa, terrarum incolas transmittit ad caelum. 'Catholicam' dicit, id est, toto orbe diffusam. 'Sanctorum communionem,' quod sequitur, id est ut cum illis sanctis, qui in hac quam suscepimus fide de praesenti saeculo ad Deum migrauerunt, societatem et spei communionem habere credamus. Si tamen recte uiuendo fidem illam teneamus, et operibus impleamus.

36. IN. Vndecimum uersum quis conposuit, aut quid in eo debeo intellegere? / 79r

RESP. Taddeus undecimum uersum conponens ait: 'Remissionem peccatorum.' Credenda est utique peccatorum remissio, quia hoc unum est remedium, quod humanum genus a sententia perpetuae mortis absoluit. Idcirco unigenitus Altissimi dignatus est et carnem sumere et crucem subire, ut nos, qui propter crimina atque peccata non poteramus euadere, sua indulgentia faceret innocentes. Et ideo inmaculatus occisus est Agnus, ut eius cruore humani generis maculae tergerentur. Ecce profunditatem mysterii! Ecce altitudinem sacramenti! Vbi mors reddit uitam, et peccantium sordes sanguine sunt innocentis mundatae. Haec autem remissio non nos ad peccatum nutrit, sed admonet, ut iam peccare timeamus, qui nos intellegimus sine

2239–2240 *Sanctam…catholicam*: the tenth verse of the Apostles' Creed.
2254–2255 *Remissionem peccatorum*: the eleventh verse of the Apostles' Creed.

uenia non posse saluari. Bonitas enim Dei munere indulgentiae suae non nos armat ad culpam, sed absoluit ad gloriam.

37. IN. Ceteris uersibus expositis, quis duodecimum conposuisset, seu etiam quid miraculi in eo habeatur, ut mihi aperias, humiliter obsecro. / 79v

RESP. Certe, frater, sicut in reliquis, ita et in hoc petitioni tuae benigno animo, prout intellego, obtemperabo. Matthias, qui ab apostolis post Iudam electus est sorte, duodecimum uersum adiecit, dicens: 'Carnis resurrectionem et uitam aeternam.' Carnem, quam in hac uita sub mortali conditione portamus, hanc resurrecturam esse inmortalem ac rationem redditurам pro consortio animae credamus. Quis enim credens Deo possit de resurrectione dubitare, cum manifestum sit hanc solam causam Christo fuisse nascendi? Quae utilitas erat, ut perpetuus carnem dignaretur adsumere, nisi ut perpetuitati carnem donaret? Quae gloria esset Dei filium crucem non refugere, mortem expetere, et perpeti sepulturam, nisi uitam mortalibus prestita resurrectione conferret? Posse hoc fieri facit diuinitas fidem, cui totum, quod uult, posse subsistit. Denique ut indubitata resurgendi exempla capiamus, ipse hic mundus amissa receptaque decoris sui specie et occidit et resurgit. Documentum nimirum futurae resurrectionis accipimus, cum commendata / 80r sulcis frumenta in stipulam suam redeunt et renouatis frondibus spoliata gelu nemora reuirescunt. Cuncta etiam, quae terra producit, aut semine aut radice multiplicata redduntur. Quae autem duritia cordis est non credere reformari hominem, cum omnia, quae facta sunt, reparentur. Vitam aeternam, quod sequitur, absque ulla dubitatione nos consecuturos credamus, si haec, quae tibi actenus exposui, firmiter teneamus ac bonis operibus fideliter conseruemus, quoniam, sicut nosti, fides sine operibus mortua est. Hoc omnibus patet.

38. Hoc est symbolum, frater mi, quod tibi exponere postulasti, cuius signaculo, sicut dictum est, in primordio fideles ab infidelibus secernuntur. Hoc est symbolum, cuius ueritas

2274–2275 *Carnis…aeternam*: the twelfth verse of the Apostles' Creed.

2283 prestita: prestitu *MS* **2291** credere reformari: *The scribe here originally wrote* credere formari *and then added a superscript correction.* **2297** tibi: ubi *MS*

unumquemque credentem efficit Christianum. Hoc est symbolum, quod et uiuentes sanctificat et mortuos reducit ad uitam, ad quam ille nos dignetur perducere, qui trinus et unus uiuit et regnat in saecula saeculorum. Amen.

<IX> INCIPIT DE DOMINICA ORATIONE

1. IN. Exposita mihi fide prout potuisti, nunc peto ut dicas mihi, si scis, Orationem Dominicam, quam Dominus noster Iesus Christus discipulos suos orare docuit.
RESP. Scio.

2. IN. Peto humiliter ut mihi illam dicas. / 80v
RESP. Prout eodem Domino miserante ualeo, qui illam docuit, faciam. Pater noster, qui es in caelis, et reliqua.

3. IN. In eadem oratione quot petitiones inueniuntur?
RESP. Septem.

4. IN. Quae est prima?
RESP. 'Sanctificetur nomen tuum.'

5. IN. Hoc, quod in capite dixisti 'Pater noster, qui es in caelis,' quomodo intellegitur?
RESP. Ibi enim inuocatio dignitatis est, dum Patrem nos habere profitemur Deum, quia omnes nos fratres sumus et Deum Patrem habemus in caelis.

6. IN. In prima petitione, quam superius dixisti, quid intellegendum est?
RESP. A Christo enim Christianus diriuatur, et ideo dum Christiani uocamur, Christi nomen tenemus et supplicamus, ut opera Christi facere ualeamus, et nomen suum per bona opera nostra in nobis sanctificetur.

7. IN. Quae est secunda petitio?

2304 As with the first half of the previous chapter, there is no direct source here. The only parallel lies with the later commentary attributed to Bruno Herbipolensis. This chapter (starting with line 2312) comprises the first part of Bruno's commentary on the *oratio dominica*. In Bruno, each question/answer is headed by a passage from the Lord's Prayer, but otherwise the dialogue format is retained and almost exactly duplicates this chapter of the *Disputatio*.

2305 mihi: tibi *MS* | potuisti: potui *MS*

RESP. 'Adueniat regnum tuum.'

8. IN. Quid ibi intellegendum est?

RESP. Oramus enim, ut Christus regnet in nobis et non diabolus; et Ecclesia Christi semper crescat, in qua regnat Deus; et dies iudicii adueniat, quia tunc diabolus in mundo regnare desistet, et Christus cum sanctis suis regnabit in aeternum.

9. IN. Quae est tertia?

RESP. 'Fiat uoluntas tua, sicut in caelo et in terra.'

10. IN. Quomodo est intellegenda?

RESP. Sicut angeli in caelo tuae uoluntati oboediunt, ita et iusti in terra faciant. Et sicut in sanctis, ita et in peccatoribus tua uoluntas impleatur.

11. IN. Quae est quarta? / 81r

RESP. 'Panem nostrum cotidianum da nobis hodie.'

12. IN. Quid in ea intellegitur?

RESP. Hoc loco panis pro omnibus cibis accipitur, de quibus cotidie uiuere debemus. Precamur etiam pro adsumptione corporis Christi. Petimus denique, ut nobis seipsum tribuat, qui est panis uiuus.

13. IN. Quae est quinta?

RESP. 'Et dimitte nobis debita nostra, sicut et nos dimittimus debitoribus nostris.'

14. IN. Quid in illa sentiendum est?

RESP. Precamur enim, ut sic dimittat nobis peccata nostra, sicut et nos dimittimus debitoribus nostris.

15. IN. Quae est sexta?

RESP. 'Et ne nos inducas in temptationem.'

16. IN. Quomodo haec intellegitur?

RESP. Non petimus ut non temptemur, quia qui non est temptatus, non est probatus. Sed precamur ut ne nos inducat in temptationem, quam sufferre non possumus.

17. IN. Quae est septima?

RESP. 'Sed libera nos a malo.'

18. IN. Quomodo est intellegenda?

RESP. Id est a diabolo, a peccato, et ab omni malo temptamento.

2331 regnat: regnet *MS*

19. IN. Amen, quod in fine est, quomodo intellegitur uel cuius lingua dicitur?
RESP. 'Amen' Hebraicae dicitur, quod Latine uere et fideliter interpretatur.

FINIT

2366 An instance of hypercorrection by the scribe. Read as an adverb ('Hebraice').

INDEX OF SCRIPTURAL CITATIONS

Citations are referenced by line number in the text of the *Disputatio*.

INDEX OF NON-SCRIPTURAL CITATIONS

Numbers in bold refer to line numbers in the text of the *Disputatio*.

TORONTO MEDIEVAL LATIN TEXTS

1 *Three Lives of English Saints*, ed. Michael Winterbottom (1972)
2 *The Gospel of Nicodemus*, ed. H.C. Kim (1973)
3 *Peter the Venerable: Selected Letters*, ed. Janet Martin (1974)
4 *A Thirteenth-Century Anthology of Rhetorical Poems*, ed. Bruce Harbert (1975)
5 *Two Alcuin Letter-Books*, ed. Colin Chase (1975)
6 *Three Latin Comedies*, ed. Keith Bate (1976)
7 *The Life of Gundulf, Bishop of Rochester*, ed. Rodney Thomson (1977)
8 *Boccaccio: In Defence of Poetry. Genealogiae deorum gentilium liber XIV*, ed. Jeremiah Reedy (1978)
9 *Bartholomaeus Anglicus: On the Properties of Soul and Body. De proprietatibus rerum libri III et IV*, ed. R. James Long (1979)
10 *Selected Sermons of Stephen Langton*, ed. Phyllis B. Roberts (1980)
11 *Philippe de Mézières' Campaign for the Feast of Mary's Presentation*, ed. William E. Coleman (1981)
12 *The Canterbury Hymnal*, ed. Gernot R. Wieland (1982)
13 *The Rule of St Benedict: The Abingdon Copy*, ed. John Chamberlin (1982)
14 *Robert Grosseteste: Templum Dei*, ed. Joseph Goering and F.A.C. Mantello (1984)
15 *The Oxford Poems of Hugh Primas and the Arundel Lyrics*, ed. C.J. McDonough (1984)
16 *Avitus: The Fall of Man. De spiritalis historiae gestis libri I–III*, ed. Daniel J. Nodes (1985)
17 *Nigel of Canterbury: Miracles of the Virgin Mary, in verse. Miracula sancte Dei genitricis virginis Marie, versifice*, ed. Jan Ziolkowski (1986)
18 *A Durham Book of Devotions*, ed. Thomas H. Bestul (1987)
19 *Speeches from the Oculus pastoralis*, ed. Terence O. Tunberg (1990)
20 *The 'Vulgate' Commentary on Ovid's Metamorphoses: The Creation Myth and the Story of Orpheus*, ed. Frank T. Coulson (1991)

21 *Richard Rolle: Emendatio vitae; Orationes ad honorem nominis Ihesu*, ed. Nicholas Watson (1995)
22 *Latin Colloquies from Pre-Conquest Britain*, ed. Scott Gwara (1996)
23 *Stella clericorum*, ed. Eric H. Reiter (1997)
24 *Fra Nicola da Milano: Collationes de beata virgine*, ed. M. Michèle Mulchahey (1997)
25 *The Fables of 'Walter of England,'* ed. Aaron E. Wright (1997)
26 *A Book of British Kings: 1200 BC–1399 AD*, ed. A.G. Rigg (2000)
27 *Saints' Lives by Walter of Châtillon: Brendan, Alexis, Thomas Becket*, ed. Carsten Wollin (2002)
28 *The Ancestry of Jesus: Excerpts from Liber generationis Iesu Christi filii Dauid filii Abraham (Matthew 1:1–17)*, ed. Greti Dinkova-Bruun (2005)
29 *The Deposition of Richard II: 'The Record and Process of the Renunciation and Deposition of Richard II' (1399) and Related Writings*, ed. David R. Carlson (2007)
30 *An Epitome of Biblical History: Glosses on Walter of Châtillon's Alexandreis 4.176–274*, ed. David Townsend (2008)
31 *The Sermons of William of Newburgh*, ed. A.B. Kraebel (2010)
32 *Peter Abelard: Historia calamitatum. Consolation to a Friend*, ed. Alexander Andrée (2015)
33 *Samuel Presbiter: Notes from the School of William de Montibus*, ed. Andrew N.J. Dunning (2016)
34 *The Disputatio puerorum: A Ninth-Century Monastic Instructional Text*, ed. Andrew Rabin and Liam Felsen (2017)